DEER STALKING

DEER STALKING

EDMUND LUXMOORE

Drawings by Briar Maxwell
Foreword by Dr Peter Delap

David & Charles
Newton Abbot   London   North Pomfret (Vt)

British Library Cataloguing in Publication Data

Luxmoore, Edmund
    Deer Stalking.
      1. Deer hunting - Great Britain
    I. title
    799.2'59'7357   SK301
    ISBN 0-7153-8063-X

Typeset by ABM Typographics Limited, Hull
and printed in Great Britain
by Redwood Burn Limited, Trowbridge and Esher
for David & Charles (Publishers) Limited
Brunel House Newton Abbot Devon

Published in the United States of America
by David & Charles Inc
North Pomfret   Vermont 05053   USA

CONTENTS

FOREWORD
Peter Delap MC, MD

To preface this book is a double embarrassment: the author knows so very much more about Highland deer than I do and I doubt my ability to convey its excellence.

Edmund Luxmoore has exceptional qualifications. As the text conveys, he became 'hooked' on deer in childhood and it has become a lifetime's addiction. Nevertheless, he found time to get a natural science degree at Cambridge and to become a successful lawyer. When a sensory disablement precluded wartime flying, he became an expert in meteorology and has transferred this knowledge to a uniquely valuable explanation of the Highland weather, so important and yet so baffling to the ordinary visitor.

In the course of this happily continuing active life, he has killed over a thousand red deer. This figure may disturb some, although they must agree that it implies invincible enthusiasm and a huge accumulation of experience: beyond which, the love of deer is evident, the whole book showing how stalking complements this love.

But how can a non-shooting man such as myself endorse such an achievement? Man spent at least a million years wandering the earth as a homeless predator: only within the last ten thousand years has he settled down to farming and only the last few generations have been drawn into the role of urbanised specialist. Do we give full recognition to those forty thousand generations, largely composed of individuals with the same sensory, aesthetic and intellectual capacities as ourselves, who refused to be defeated? Living from hand to mouth, without any back-up resources, every individual had to be a consistently successful hunter, in the face of sickness, blizzard or injury, for at least twenty years, if his loved ones were to survive. No wonder that this most ancient of imperatives is easily revived, even though some of us, of necessity, sublimate it with a camera.

This was my case: a few bloody and unorthodox encounters with deer in my youth, reinforced by penury, convinced me that I would never make a good stalker. Later, I found myself all too often at the wrong end of small-arms fire and too many brave young men died at my knees. One conviction that emerged was that, setting aside the potential for intellectual anguish peculiar to the human condition, the mortal wound brought little pain: physical suffering was usually proportionate to the diffuseness and persistence of trauma. I had the salutary experience, literally in my own bones, of moving across rough country with stiffening wounds. A further realisation was the increasing unpleasantness of re-exposure to small-arms fire: some deer, especially in England, are wounded four or five times before they succumb.

The writer of this book reiterates in print, and carries fully into practice, the paramount duty of the stalker to minimise suffering. He was fortunate in serving a long apprenticeship with Highland and Lake District experts and in never losing his sense of meticulous dedication.

Stalking, throughout the British Isles, is now becoming available to a much wider social spectrum than heretofore. Pockets of die-hard snobbery persist, usually led by individuals whose acquaintance would be burdensome anyway. What is vital is that the new adherents should accept the necessity of a gradual and uncompetitive approach to the art.

A valid analogy is with Alpine climbing. Pre-war, this was largely the prerogative of university types and carried its own snobberies and restrictions. Since then, men from all walks of life have united to advance and revitalise the sport. Nowadays, to become a competent climber involves the mastery of complex equipment as well as physical fitness. The expenditure of time, money and sheer effort will be comparable, whether you end up with a photograph of one of the tougher Chamonix Aiguilles or an elegant Highland head hanging on your wall. The extreme limits of modern climbing are best left to the man with a built-in death wish, and the young stalker of today should likewise beware of the farther fringes of his sport.

There are still many men of the calibre of Edmund Luxmoore, with lifelong access to the best of stalking, who remain cheerfully uncompetitvie, largely content to cull rubbishy heads and usually in agreement that the 'wild' Highland eight-pointer makes the most aesthetically satisfactory trophy of all. Commercial pressures are increasingly at work to inflate the prestige of sheer size and the cost of securing a really big head has passed beyond all reason. Results are measured (and paid for) purely in terms of cubic capacity. Even those able to compete in this league should be careful. There is a brisk trade nowadays in English park stags for export northwards and subsequent skilled presentation to the unwary and wealthy novice. One feels that the promoters of such schemes would themselves, in a different context, import an alien beauty of sixteen stone in preference to a compatriot of half the weight.

There are still plenty of genuinely wild Highland deer available and this book should help greatly in their defence, if they are to retain their place as the greatest material and spiritual asset upon those impoverished hills. Were Landseer alive today he would paint not a twelve-pointer bayed by staghounds but a yearling hind trapped between computers and filing cabinets by grim men in bowler hats.

We must be grateful for scientific research, especially when, as in Dr Iain Colquhoun's work summarised herein, it is combined with a genuine long-standing love of deer. In times of severe financial pressures, such as these, it is invaluable to know that deer and sheep fill complementary ecological niches and are not in direct competition. A few other scientists have studied deer with the same loving but dispassionate eye: sadly, for most, they remain mere experimental material from which to extract a PhD, before a quick retreat to a softer environment.

The productions of the various organisations now competing for the deer's shrinking habitat must inevitably be antagonistic to them. Current forestry techniques inexorably conflict with most forms of multiple-purpose land use: but the electronic letter and the micro-dot newspaper are just around the next technological corner and the rush to produce wood-pulp will not last forever. The red stag was on the hill before the Sitka spruce and will be there when disease and desuetude have removed that alien.

The protagonists of deer-farming are currently keen and persuasive, but the reality is inevitably as harsh and unromantic as the financial pressures involved. The few stags allowed to reach maturity for stud purposes will inevitably be subjected to the annual removal of their antlers while still in velvet. This is unavoidably a shattering physical and psychological shock to the animal, but the end-product can be exported to the Orient as an aphrodisiac at a grotesquely inflated price.

This book is written in the hope that it will bring informed and active new recruits to the stalking scene. If so, the work of the Red Deer Commission may become less arduous. This body has been criticised for local over-kills, so there should still be a niche for the enthusiastic (and unpaid) amateur. Meanwhile, we should not be over-critical of that body, whose members are, after all, in spite of muddy boots and bloody hands, bureaucrats with norms to meet and time-sheets to fill in: but, on the facts and figures set out, is there really a surplus of deer, valuable asset as they are?

In spite of all the pressures upon him and upon his beloved deer, the writer of this book remains a serene and forward-looking optimist, remarkably free from the testy nostalgia of the usual sporting raconteur: this is a splendidly realistic account of stalking today and a lead into the future. I have kept you from it too long.

I

WHAT IT IS ALL ABOUT

My introduction to stalking was entirely fortuitous. When I was ten, my parents decided to take my brother and myself to Mull to fish and play about in boats: a friend of my father's had offered him a day's stalking, so he was going equipped for that. At the last moment, my brother fell ill and, after much discussion, it was decided that my father should take me, as planned, my mother staying at home with my brother, hoping he might get well enough to travel in a few days and join us. In the event, this turned out not to be so. My father was about to cancel his day's stalking, but I begged him so much to go on with it and allow me to come with him, assuring him that I could do the necessary walking that, in the end, he explained the situation to his host and I was taken on my first day's stalking.

Of the day, I remember little, except that I was absolutely determined that I should walk, because everybody had said I could not. I was determined, too, that I should not let my father down. I could not see the deer, because they are by no means easy for inexperienced people to see on the hill, their camouflage being extraordinarily good, and I could not manage the telescopes which my father and the stalker had; but, when the final approach was made, the stalker beckoned me up and, approaching very cautiously,

Three-year-old stag in velvet (July). He is too young to have a good 'spread' but has the making of a good head

I peeped over the top, and did see my father shoot the stag. I managed somehow to walk back to the car and so arrived back at the hotel, but I am told I was so tired that I was quite unable to eat anything and went to bed and slept for fourteen hours, after which, I woke up considering myself a fully-fledged deer stalker!

That was well over fifty years ago and, although I have found there is a great deal more to it than I thought then, I have stalked every autumn and most winters since that memorable day, except for a few in the War. I am very grateful to my father and to the old stalker who, I am sure (looking back on it), found a small stag handy that day and took it. I can still picture him as the most venerable old man with an enormous white beard, which impressed me greatly as a small boy, but must have been a serious disadvantage when stalking. The other thing that impressed me on being taken into his house, where we were received with the greatest courtesy which one always finds in stalkers, was that the table was set for the stalker and his wife with the usual spoons and forks, accompanied by a set of false teeth at each place: an admirable idea, if one comes to think of it, but one I have never seen followed again!

Deer stalking, like salmon fishing is, in fact, little as I thought it in those early days, a thing which one goes on learning more and more about every time one goes out: there is no such person as a fully-fledged stalker who knows it all. But, on the other hand, a little knowledge of what is going on helps a great deal in the enjoyment of a day on the hill, while knowledge of the habits of deer and their place in the ecology of the Highlands helps not only in the proper management of deer forests, but also in the understanding of the necessity for deer stalking at all in these days when so much emphasis, quite rightly, is placed upon conservation.

It is with these two aspects in mind that this book is written. The reader will find that the remainder of this chapter, and Chapters 2, 3 and 4, deal with the deer themselves, with their requirements for survival, and with their place in the general ecology and economy of the Highlands. Chapters 5 to 10 deal with the actual stalking, its principles and practices, and the equipment required, while the last two chapters are accounts of stalking, by way of illustration.

Those readers who are merely interested in the actual stalking may care to start at Chapter 5. Such a suggestion may seem to imply something illogical in the layout but, really, a knowledge of the habits and requirements of the deer themselves is the most basic part of our study, and helps us to understand the stalking practice: hence, it is put first.

One only has to look at coats of arms, posters, advertisements and so on, all of which are covered with red deer and stags' heads, to see what an extraordinary fascination they have had for people down the ages.

Red deer (which hereafter are referred to as 'deer', other sorts being given their full names) are our largest surviving land mammals. It is surprising, in these circumstances, how little scientific investi-

Wolves

gation has been carried out into deer in this country until recent times, when it has received an added impetus from the interest in deer-farming.

In addition to their fascination, they have always provoked much emotion, either because they used to be, for many years, the 'sport of kings' and, accordingly, protected by vicious poaching laws which made for a sense of jealousy about deer, which is still ingrained into a section of the country folk; or because, at the other end of the scale, there is the sentimental approach to deer, which one may call the 'Bambi' attitude. Both these attitudes militate against the killing of deer so that, at first sight, it might seem to be wrong. Let us consider it further.

As with all natural problems, one of the first and best methods of approach is to consider what nature decrees. Deer were the natural prey of a number of larger predators in this country, wolf, bear, lynx and wolverine and, to a lesser extent, small predators, such as

Lynx

foxes, which prey on the calves only. The deer's reproduction rate, therefore, allows for a substantial cull by these predators and, as man has removed all except foxes and a few smaller predators, the same cull must be taken in some other way in order to preserve the deer herds in the state and numbers in which nature intended them to be. The right and sensible way to take this cull is by stalking, and the object of stalking is to do it humanely, and for the benefit of the deer herds, by selective shooting.

People naturally wonder whether stalking can be carried on in conjunction with the other activites of the countryside. Since the introduction of sheep to the Highlands, following the Highland

A pair of wolverines

Clearances, described so well in Duff Hart Davis's book *Monarchs of the Glen*, published in 1978, sheep have only been a paying proposition on the Highland hills for short periods, and there have been many times when they have been at a discount. At present, they probably only pay by reason of the substantial subsidy; and the statistics for the last twenty years, published by the North of Scotland School of Agriculture, show that in only one year in five did the average profit of Highland sheep farms exceed the average sheep subsidy paid to such farms.

From the economic point of view, if deer and sheep can run together, the profitability of the Highlands is greatly increased, as is employment in an area where employment is at a premium. The compatibility of sheep and deer on the open hills is examined more closely in Chapter 4, but I have been able to trace over 80 scientific and semi-scientific works on multiple grazing by ungulates, and all those which come to any conclusion say that different species do not compete, but are complementary. A number, done in Africa, show clearly that, where some species were removed to encourage one other, the reverse effect has occurred, because plants grazed by the removed species have grown too much and swamped those favoured by the species desired.

Additionally, deer themselves provide a very welcome source of foreign capital. Venison finds a ready sale on the Continent and much is now exported, while stalking can readily be let to foreign sportsmen: so one can say that, for each stag shot in the season, something between £200 and £600 in foreign currency is obtained, taking into account appropriate figures for sale of venison, rent, tourism and so on. Very healthy and skilful recreation is to be had as well, and it is not surprising to find that, in spite of the feelings against killing deer mentioned above, stalking is now far more popular than it has ever been, and the number of deer forests has risen from six in 1830 to more than 600 now.

A recent article in *The Field* by a leading sporting-estates agency said that the value of deer forests has increased by the astonishing figure of 1,600% between 1965 and 1980.

The proper management of deer as one of the natural resources of the Highlands is of far more importance than the mere whim of a sportsman, or the desire to have a trophy which can be hung upon the ancestral wall.

The position of deer-farming should also be mentioned. We have already seen that, because of the natural reproduction rate of deer, coupled with the removal by man of the main predators, the culling of deer is essential for the preservation of the deer herds, and this can be done so as to improve the herds. However, there may be some who argue that the culling should be done under farm conditions.

Very valuable work has been done by the Rowett Research Institute, near Aberdeen, run by the Department of Agriculture for Scotland, and in 1974 they published an excellent book *Farming the Red Deer*. This received wide publicity all over the world and, by 1978, over 800 deer farms had been established in New Zealand, and were considered such a valuable asset to the economy that live hinds were fetching, on average, £800 each, the meat being exported to Europe. The Germans expected to establish 300 by early 1979; but we, in this country, have lagged far behind so that, at the beginning of 1979, there were only 10 or 12 farms going on a commercial basis.

The lag in this country may not, however, be entirely fortuitous, for the red deer herds can exist in a truly wild state in the Highlands of Scotland, as well as on the hills of the Lake District in England, and possibly elsewhere. There are wild deer on Exmoor, in the New Forest and in the forests of East Anglia, but there they require considerably more preservation.

Young stag and hinds, with one yearling and a calf

From the point of view of the conservationist, and also the deer, it is far better that they should lead a truly wild life on the hills, and end it by a clean, quick shot. The alternatives are to be farmed, driven into a slaughter house (however well run) and killed there or, because of the absence of predators, live out their lives to old age and then die a very slow and lingering death from semi-starvation. This is the fate of the deer in the winter when they get old, for they lose their teeth and cannot get enough nourishment. They are extraordinarily disease- and parasite-resistant, so that very few die naturally from anything but old age and/or starvation.

Those who are vegetarian, because they object to killing for meat, deserve respect, but have they ever thought of what this country would be like if the killing of animals was forbidden? There would be no farm animals in our fields; there would be no deer, because they would increase far too much and do too much damage due to overcrowding; and there would be no eggs or milk because, nature being what it is, it is impossible to breed hens only or cows only so that, if one wants eggs and milk, the male surplus in either case must be killed off. There would be no green grass fields, because there would be no use for them!

The merits or cruelty of battery- or factory-farming are not the subject of this book, except to mention that, in order to farm deer, very high costs of fencing are involved. Since deer are considerable jumpers, and very adept at getting through holes, fences must be at least twice as high as the ordinary stock fence, and in much better condition. This being so, the tendency is to contract the sizes of the farms as much as practicable, so as to reduce the proportionate cost of fencing, and the trend must, therefore, be to get nearer and nearer to factory farming conditions. At the outset, the wild nature of the deer would probably preclude actual factory-farming, but it is remarkable, in such experimental farms as are going, to see how rapidly the deer will suffer living inside, even though it cannot be what nature intended.

The fact of the matter, therefore, is that, from the point of view of the deer and the conservationist alike, deer ought to live on the open hills where they belong. This is possible even in these crowded islands.

Finally, a word on a very pleasant and entertaining adjunct to stalking, deer photography. This is a specialised subject on its own, and has really nothing to do with deer management, but it must be appreciated that it cannot be the sole object of maintaining a forest. A forest could not be maintained purely for the photographing of deer for two simple reasons: first, a proper cull of the deer must be taken, as we have seen and, second, unless deer are stalked and shot, they will readily become much too tame and, in that case, would be too apt to raid the low-ground crops. That, in turn, would lead to slaughter or poaching. Stalking is necessary to keep the deer in a truly wild state, when the art and pleasure of photographing a genuinely wild animal remains. If one wishes to photograph tame deer, it is better done in one of the deer parks.

2

FOOD

Before considering the proper management of a deer forest, it is essential to study the preferences, requirements and necessities of the deer themselves. If the necessities are not present, the enterprise must fail. The degree of success, on the other hand, will depend largely on the provision of the requirements, in order of preference, either by nature, in the shape of topography or vegetation, or by the proprietor of the forest himself, in the shape of artificial feeds, the improvement of grazing and the provision of shelter belts and the like.

Deer were intended by nature to live mainly in wooded forests and are, therefore, browsers as well as grazers; they do both in their natural state in the great forests of central Europe. One of the most remarkable and rapid pieces of adaptation is the change which has taken place in the deer of the Highlands of Scotland when, following the clearance of the trees in the 18th and 19th centuries, they adapted themselves to life on the open hill. In the process, they have become considerably smaller than their predecessors and cousins now living in the forested areas of central Europe, though there is no genetic change. They have achieved this adaptation so remarkably well over the last 200 years or so that they are now able to live on the open hillside without the provision of additional food.

It will be said at once that deer have been fed in the Highlands ever since stalking became popular, about 100 years ago: that is true, but it is not a necessity for the deer. There are many forests where it is still not practised and, even where it is, feeding is limited to stags. This limit is imposed not by the proprietor but by the hinds themselves, since they prefer to remain on their habitual territory, reasonably high up in the hills; whereas, feeding is nearly always done, for practical reasons of transport, in some glen or valley near the stalker's house, which will always be situated low down. In general, the stags will come down to this and become regular feeders in the winter, but the hinds will not. Thus, basically, the hinds can and do survive on the open hill without additional feeding, and it would be very surprising if the male of the species could not manage in the same way: they can and do on a number of forests.

That is not to say that feeding for stags in winter is not an advantageous practice: indeed, it is. The stags become very run-down in the autumn after the rut, and additional feeding builds them up in the winter, enabling them to grow better bodies and larger heads. This, in effect, reverses the trend of the rapid adaptation from larger woodland-living animals to smaller animals living on the open hill; but it must be remembered that, once it has been started and the trend reversed, it becomes a necessity for the stags rather than an

Hinds grazing and resting

initial preference. Thus, a stag which has been fed over two or three winters grows larger both in head and body than its brother without additional feeding, with the result that, when the rut comes round, the fed stag will be heavier and in a position to hold more hinds, and so will become more run-down. It will need more additional feeding than ever the next winter, both to build up its larger body and to restore the strength which it has lost. It is that stag, and not its smaller brother, which will die in a hard winter if feeding is suddenly withdrawn.

If winter feeding is undertaken, therefore, it is essential that it be continued from year to year. As above, nearly all hinds and many stags live entirely on the open hill so it clearly provides all the food necessities of deer at all times of the year and, for the most part, the hills of Scotland are grossly undergrazed. It is well known that grass which is cut stays green much longer than that which is left to flower, go to seed and wither, and the quality of the grazing would be greatly improved by further grazing. So that there is, in fact, no shortage of food for the deer, except under extreme snow conditions when they cannot get at it but, even then, they have long legs and are very adept at scraping away the snow, knowing instinctively where they will find the grazing which they require. This, incidentally, is of great value to sheep, which are often seen following the deer in the snow, taking advantage of the scraping.

Most people will find it remarkable but it is, nevertheless, one of the scientific facts which has come out of recent studies of deer for the purposes of deer-farming, that the appetite of deer decreases in the winter. One would think that, because it is colder, they would require a greater intake of food. This, however, is not so: the intake of food is required in the spring and summer when there is most grazing available, and then they build up reserves of fat to carry them through the winter, as well as, in the case of stags, through the rut.

The decrease of appetite during winter is not quite so surprising when one thinks about the matter a bit more deeply, since, in the case of the hinds, they do not need to provide milk for the previous summer's calf after September, although they may well go on providing a small amount of milk well up to the end of the year. It had been thought by stalkers for many years that milk over this period was essential for the calves, but recent research for deer farming has shown that calves can be satisfactorily weaned after eight weeks, and are always so weaned under farming conditions. That would mean that they could be weaned on the hill in August but, under hill conditions, this is probably too soon, for they cannot get there the special foods provided in a farm. Even under hill conditions, milk ceases to be essential after another month, so that calves could be weaned by the hinds, at any rate, by the end of September.

The quantity of milk supplied after September is small, while the embryo calf for the following year develops very slowly over the winter period, being very little heavier in a hind shot in mid-February than one shot in December. The time of rapid development of the embryo is April and May. This slow early development of the embryo is probably also associated with the ability of a hind in poor condition and, therefore, unlikely to be able to rear a calf that year, to re-absorb the embryo into its system.

So far as the stags are concerned, they do lose a great deal of condition in the rut, but there is much of the summer vegetation still available at the end of the rut, and they pick up quite rapidly at first and, thereafter, remain in more or less static condition until they cast their horns the following April. They require additional

Young stags: two sparring as they often do

food to grow their new horns (or antlers as they are more properly, but seldom, called in Scotland) but they never really get back into bodily condition until, probably, July, when there is ample vegetation.

Anyone looking at the brown and apparently dead condition of the hills in winter will wonder what sustenance they provide. Deer do seem, however, to be able to digest a great deal of the coarse, dead vegetation, provided that the bacteria in their rumen are in good condition. These bacteria require a little green food to keep them going, so that some green food is essential to deer, but only little is necessary.

A further unexplained but definite fact is that stags eat coarser dead vegetation in the winter than hinds, so they, especially, are able to deal with the dead 'deer' grass (*Molinia* and/or *Scirpus cespitosus*). This is a great advantage to the hill because, when the snow comes, the dead grass gets pushed down and smothers the new grass, putting it back in growth in the spring. If the deer have removed the dead grass, the spring green will appear earlier.

Because deer graze the hills, there is a tendency to think of grass as their staple food but, if it is remembered that deer are by nature forest dwellers and, therefore, browsers, it will come as no surprise to find that, over the winter at any rate, their staple food is the heather and other dwarf shrubs found on the hill. Dr Iain Colquhoun, in his very thorough investigation mentioned in Chapter 4, gives a figure of about 40% heather and other dwarf shrubs over the winter months, about 15% sedges, about 20%, or possibly slightly more, mosses, and 25%, or possibly slightly less, grasses. I, myself, am able to confirm that, in particularly snowy conditions, the deer turn almost entirely to heather, for I have been compelled by the Red Deer Commission to shoot a large number of stags in snow conditions in the late winter and spring, which, when gralloched, showed that the stomach content was very largely heather.

It is easy to see from the above analysis of the intake of deer in winter that they can get quite enough green stuff for the small requirements of their digestive system from the mosses, which mostly remain green in the winter, and from the heather, which also, to a greater or lesser extent, remains green in the winter, particularly when it has been covered by snow.

In 1979, after the very heavy snow storms of January and February, it was quite remarkable to see, in the first week of March, the pattern on the hills where the snow drifts had lain. Even up to a considerable height, everywhere the snow had melted, the heather was green and apparently growing well; whereas, where the snow had been blown clear from the tops of the hillocks, the heather had been frosted, and was quite brown. The pattern was a mosaic of green and brown, the divisions between the two colours being quite sharp and distinct. Even the grass had begun to grow in the places under the snow, but only where the hills had not been clear of snow.

In spring, deer eat the young shoots of bracken. The intake of bracken is not large, but the eating of the young shoots does have a weakening effect, at least, bracken being otherwise an entire waste of space on the hills, and a bad harbourer of ticks.

Much could be done to improve the hills by up-grading the quality of the grazing, but great care would have to be taken to see that it is the winter grazing which is improved: there is ample in the summer.

The grass of the Highlands is mostly of the 'deer grass' type, which goes an orange-brown in the autumn, giving the much-admired autumn tints to the hills. It is of poor nutritional value in winter although, as mentioned, the deer do manage to get something from it. The most nutritional grassland is 'agrosto-festucetum', but this is entirely dormant in the winter, and as it only forms a very small fraction of the herbage of the Scottish Highlands, any residue of this grass left in autumn is quickly eaten by the sheep and, therefore, forms no substantial contribution to winter grazing.

The *Agrostis/Festuca* grasses are the very green grasses normally found on hummocks and other well-drained places, looking like lawn grass (as indeed it is), and any gardener knows the more a lawn is cut, the more it comes. It forms a very valuable nutrient in summer and always gets well grazed. It is about the last of the herbage to start growing in the spring, since the hills do not get warm until much later than the average lowland lawn. Because it grows on the dry hummocks, the sheep use it for their night sleeping ground and, because it forms such a small proportion of the total coverage, what, in fact, happens in spring is that some of the older ewes take up residence on the agrostis knolls and protect them as their own territories from all other sheep, many of which, such as the hoggs returning from winter, require it much more but probably never get at it until early June.

For winter grazing for both sheep and deer, the importance of heather and other dwarf shrubs cannot be overstressed. Much grazing in the Highlands has been ruined by wrong burning of heather. 'Deer grass' is far more resistant to burning than heather or the agrostis grass and, therefore, any large areas of burning or fierce fires result in the replacement of heather and agrostis grass by 'deer grass'.

It is very easy to set alight a patch of heather, but it requires a great deal of controlling to keep the burning area small enough and, in the past, the areas burnt have been far too big. Only very small areas of heather should be burnt, if heather is to regenerate.

3
HABITAT

Food, which we have already considered, is, of course, the most important necessity for all wild animals: the next in order of importance is probably habitat. It is certainly extremely important for deer and, going back to their woodland ancestry, it will be readily appreciated that shelter is of prime importance.

Although the Highland deer have adapted themselves to life on the hills, they still require shelter from strong winds and prolonged periods of rain, and they achieve this by moving into the lee of steep hills or into small corries where the wind goes over the top of them. They will go considerable distances to find good shelter, and they have a quite extraordinary ability for predicting weather in advance of its actual arrival.

Again, I think of early March 1979 when, following the clearance of the snow on the higher hills up to about 2000ft (600m), deer had moved out to take advantage of the green heather mentioned earlier. On the night of a Tuesday/Wednesday, no snow or particularly high winds were forecast, but large numbers of deer came back on to the lower ground. On Thursday, Friday and Saturday, blizzard conditions with gale force winds occurred, which the deer had clearly anticipated.

Young stags with horns half grown

On the whole, deer do not live in very large herds and, under
normal conditions, a herd of over 40 is the exception rather than
the rule. However, when strong winds and rain are coming or are
present, deer collect up into large herds of perhaps several hundred,
and this gives them additional shelter and warmth from each other.

Snow does not affect deer nearly as much as rain, provided it is
dry: dry snow settles on their coats and they shake it off without any
moisture penetrating. Indeed, when they are lying, they very often
do not worry to get up and shake snow off, and it probably acts to
keep in the heat to some extent. Prolonged slushy snow or rain

finally penetrates the coat and causes cooling: showers or short periods of rain do not penetrate the undercoat and are shaken off.

Provided the weather is not too bad or the wind too strong, the deer like to spend the day on an open hill-face where they get a good view of approaching danger (the dividing line between too strong a wind or not is somewhere in the lower force four, depending on the temperature). In those conditions, they will spend the day near the top of the slope, moving down into the wind at night, so that they can smell any danger ahead of them. They prefer a constant wind, and are always uneasy where the wind is frequently changing, a situation often found on very steep lee slopes which, from the map, one would think would provide admirable shelter but are, in fact, subject to eddies of wind, first one way and then another. A southern aspect is also favoured, for deer like the sunshine, except in really hot weather.

Thus, the ideal forest will have good open slopes with good visibility for fine weather, and good shelter for bad weather; and it should have these at various levels for the different times of year. Alternatively, an area with little knolls is also favoured, because the deer can get a view in fine weather by going on top of the knolls, and shelter in the small valleys between them. They do not like the shelter to be too enclosed where they cannot see out, such as deep ravines, which are seldom popular.

If the slopes are too open, the stalking will be difficult, but that is discussed later under 'Stalking', as are the individual localities where deer are to be found on any particular day, and other matters of more localised detail of the ground.

Apart from the rutting season, stags and hinds do not live together normally. Calves, of course, remain with their mothers for the first year, and second-year stags (called 'knobbers') with a fair proportion of stags in their third year, generally remain with the hinds. Apart from that, the sexes tend to separate. There seems to be no actual fight between them, and no real antipathy one to the other, for if, in the course of movement or weather conditions, they come together, they remain quite happily together, possibly for days, possibly for weeks. However, in general, though it is only a generalisation and there are many exceptions, the sexes separate for the whole of the year except for the rutting season. It is the hinds which remain on their own ground and the stags which go off

Family group—hind, yearling and calf—in winter

elsewhere, often travelling quite large distances to known 'stag forests', where they tend to congregate.

There seems to be no particular differentiation between the type of ground suitable for a stag forest and that known as hind ground where the hinds stay, except that, from time immemorial, the stag forests have been such, and the migration routes (for that is what is, in effect, taken by stags after the rut to reach the stag forests) are well known and established: though at the present time, owing to much forestry plantation, some of these routes have been barred to the stags.

There have been many instances of stags coming up against new forestry fences where they simply walk up and down the fences and, in hard weather, have died in large numbers. Other instances occur where there is a long fence barring an ancestral migration route, which results in a build-up of the stag population on the open side of the fence: often, there are almost waves of stags coming against the fence and 'bouncing back' into the forest on the open side. The migration is by no means the mass migration, now well known through the excellent films of natural history, of caribou in Canada or reindeer in Lapland but it is a general drift after the rut, usually in small parties, or even singly.

The hinds, as has been noted, tend to stay much more in one place and, in general, they will do their best to remain within a reasonable radius of where they were born. Their territorial instinct may well account for part of their reluctance to come down to artificial feeding.

All deer tend to move higher in summer, probably to get away from the flies but here, again, it is the stags which move furthest, and certainly try to go highest, for two reasons, first, that they are not encumbered by their new-born calves, and, second, that they are then growing their horns, which are very sensitive and very subject to irritation by flies.

A large forest will always have some stags, whether it is predominantly hind or stag country, in the season when stag shooting is open, namely, from 1st July to 20th October. But, for the tenant who just wants to take a short period of stalking, it is important to enquire or to ascertain somehow whether the forest is a stag or hind forest, for the purely hind forests will only have stags in the rut.

In the rut, of course, those forests with plenty of hinds will get the pick of the big stags, for stags travel great distances, if necessary, to get hinds, although a particular stag that has held hinds in a particular place will nearly always come back to exactly the same lot of hinds and place the following year. I have known quite a lot of instances of easily recognisable stags doing just that. I particularly remember one big, one-horned stag, which seemed to have a charmed life, coming back to exactly the same hillock, to which it drove a herd of hinds from round about, on almost exactly the same day each year for three years, on a forest I had just after the war. I am sure it had been shot at several times and missed, as it kept a much better look-out than a rutting stag normally does, and something quite unforeseen always went wrong with the stalks we had in the first two years. It also had the unusual trait that at the first sign of danger, it went off and left the hinds. It took me five stalks and three years to defeat it! It left behind two generations of small one-horned stags which had to be gradually mopped up.

However, that is a digression: we now turn to what is perhaps the most important aspect of the habitat, namely, the number of deer which the ground will carry. Obviously, no proper planning of a deer forest can be carried out until the carrying capacity has been ascertained. It is, of course, acknowledged that deer move sub-stantially, particularly the stags as mentioned above but, neverthe-less, the average number of deer which the ground will carry must be discovered before proper plans can be laid. No farmer starts stocking his farm until he knows what stock it will carry. That is the starting point: he may later improve the grazing and so increase the carrying capacity but, until he knows the original carrying capacity, he cannot even decide how much he will have to spend on improve-ments.

Strangely enough, until recent investigations into deer-farming, there has been remarkably little information available on this vital aspect of deer-forest management. This has, in part it is true, been due to the erroneous impression that deer and sheep compete on the same grazing. That aspect of the matter is discussed in a subsequent chapter on deer and sheep, where also will be considered what allowance should be made to the figures quoted below if the land is under joint grazing by deer and sheep.

One of the first official pronouncements on carrying capacity of hill land is to be found in the first report of an investigation by the Rowett Research Institute and the Hill Farming Research Organisa-tion, published in 1974 by the Department of Agriculture and Fisheries for Scotland, and entitled *Farming the Red Deer*. There, the area investigated was situated in Aberdeenshire, on the east coast, and consisted of various types of land.

The areas, which are described variously as typical Highland hill land, or unimproved hill grazing, were stocked at 1 deer per 4 acres (1·6ha) to 1 deer per 10 acres (4ha), and it was noted that their carrying capacity for deer stock was quite impressive. On the lower ranges, where the stocking ratio had been 1 to 4, it was observed that there was little evidence of change in the characteristics of the herbage, indicating that here the stocking intensity was well below the carrying capacity. Of the two other hill grazings, which were stocked at a ratio of 1 deer per 10 acres (4ha), it is observed that they had not been subject to any grazing pressure at all at this stocking ratio, and that there was no immediately discernible change in the nature of the grazings, in terms of their botanical composition. It is observed that the two grazings could well have carried considerably more stock.

Aberdeenshire, it is true, is the driest part of the Highlands, and this will, of course, have some bearing on the matter. However, in 1976, the Highlands and Islands Development Board purchased the deer forest of Rahoy, on the West Coast, for the purpose of setting up an experimental deer farm there. In this project, they were advised by the Red Deer Commission and by the Nature Conservancy. This, in contrast to Aberdeenshire, is one of the wettest parts of Scotland but, in spite of that, various articles or press releases have appeared from time to time since its purchase, indicating that, on the hill land, the stocking rate would be 1 deer per 4 acres (1·6ha). There is also low ground but that, apparently, is to be used for rearing the calves on a more intensive basis, the deer on the hill land living there without any, or any substantial, additional feeding. It is to be noted that, in one of these press articles, the Board states that the forest ground is lacking in heather, which, as we have already seen, is the staple food of deer in winter.

Following the 1974 report on deer-farming just mentioned, a few deer farms have been established in Scotland, but their number is believed not to exceed ten or twelve at the time of writing, and they are mostly intensive farms, where a substantial amount of additional feed is put in. However, one, in particular, is farming on a 1000 acre (400ha) hill unit, where, according to an article in the *Scottish Farmer* of August 1978, the deer, once put on to the hill unit at the age of twenty weeks, receive no additional feeding except a little hay in storm conditions, and it is said that there will be, on the one thousand acres of hill land, a three-hundred-hind herd. Taking into account stags and followers, this means approximately 400 deer on 1000 acres, or 1 deer to 2½ acres (1·0ha).

Taking the above figures as being accurate, and based on the best scientific knowledge available at this time, it seems that deer forests could be stocked at the rate of 1 deer per 4 acres (1·6ha). Many deer forests carry far less stock, but the evidence above indicates that few, if any, forests are stocked up to anything like their carrying capacity, when it is remembered that the deer stock of Scotland is estimated to be about 250,000 deer, spread over an area of more than seven million acres (nearly three million ha).

It is safe to say that there must be very few forests indeed where the stocking ratio could not be 1 deer per 10 acres (4ha) at least and, since deer are such a very valuable commodity or asset in the economics of the Highlands now, forests ought to be stocked up to their reasonable maximum carrying capacity in the national interest, making allowance, of course, for the sheep stock, as discussed later.

That nearly every forest is substantially understocked is confirmed by the fact that, 150 years ago, the Highlands carried a very much larger stock of assorted animals, though probably less deer, than they carry now, and secondly, by examination of the grazing itself. Very little evidence of over-grazing can be found and, on most forests, there is substantial evidence of under-grazing.

To take but one instance of this, one finds on the Pennines of England, where the sheep-stocking rate on the heather is 3 sheep per acre (0·4ha), normally, and where there is a substantial number of grouse (which eat heather almost entirely), burning has to be done to keep the heather in control, and it is only when the sheep stock goes greatly over 3 per acre that one gets the close-cropped appearance of over-grazing. That is seldom to be seen in the Highlands though: where the heather is at its extreme range of height, it is, of course, stunted. That is different from being over-grazed. Grazing of heather is far better for the heather than burning, because it does not destroy the roots and produces vigorous new growth much more quickly, in just the same way as garden shrubs do when pruned.

Burning has to be very carefully controlled, otherwise the roots will be burnt and, in that case, the deer grass, which gives the hills the typical golden appearance in autumn, will come instead of the heather. The same take-over by deer grass occurs if the area burnt is anything but small, because the grass seed is much more easily carried by the wind than that of heather.

Of course, it will be said that the above-quoted examples of stocking rates apply where a minimal amount of hay is provided in storm conditions but, even so, and allowing for the fact that winter or spring are the critical times, there is still a great deal of difference between 1 deer per 4 acres (1·6ha) and 1 deer per 10 acres (4ha). Thus, the latter figure must allow, under practically all conditions, a safe margin. This is even more evident when it is remembered that the quoted area of forest is always measured on a flat map, which is a projection of the land on to the horizontal, that is to say, a bird's-eye view. In practice, much of the land is very steep and the actual surface area is, therefore, very much greater. For instance, even at a slope of 1 in 1 (45°), which is by no means steep as Highland hills go, the actual surface area is 45% greater than the area shown on the map.

4
SHEEP AND DEER

As has been pointed out in Chapter I, sheep and deer are frequently found on the hill in close proximity to each other, but I have never seen, in more than fifty years' stalking, and have never heard from stalkers, on frequent enquiry, of any serious antipathy between the two species. Indeed, they seem to get on perfectly well together on the hill and, not only do they show no sign of antipathy to or of fighting each other but, also, no sign of attempting to avoid each other. Thus, on the usual rules of nature, there must be a strong presumption that they do not seriously compete with each other. This does not apply to fallow deer, which dislike sheep.

On the other hand, however, the view is held among Highlanders in the countryside that sheep and deer do not get on together. It may be asked how this arises, if it is not correct since, usually, country-men know what they are talking about, especially in country matters. But the position here is not as easy as that, because, for the most part, sheep and deer interests have become separated and, therefore, those whose primary interest is in deer have little interest in the sheep and those, such as the tenant farmers or crofters, whose primary interest is in the sheep, have no interest in the deer. If one wants to blame something for any misfortune then, of course, it is obvious that one blames the thing in which one has little or no interest.

The matter, in the case of the deer, is further aggravated by the fact that the presence of sheep undoubtedly makes stalking considerably more difficult, and no stalker of experience will be unable to recall many occasions when a stalk was spoilt by sheep. One can entirely understand this attitude, especially on the part of the professional stalker, whose job it is to get a stag for his employer or guest, as the case may be, but it is really entirely a wrong attitude. The sport of stalking is the ability to overcome the difficulties of getting a shot.

The Victorians, hampered originally by highly inaccurate rifles, and then spurred on by intense competition between different proprietors who so much wanted to say that they had the largest bag, or got the best heads, disliked sheep. They disliked anything that made the stalking more difficult or, as we should now say, more

Stags just casting velvet (August)

sporting. Nowadays, if one merely wants to get a large number of deer, then one should deer-farm. Be that as it may, a great many forests were denuded of sheep to improve the stalking and, because some people had done it, others felt they must follow suit to keep up with their neighbours.

It seemed only natural, too, that, because sheep and deer both ate the herbage of the hills, they must compete and, therefore, the quality of the deer would be improved by removing the sheep. On the one hand, the theory that sheep were bad for deer grew up and, on the other hand, the tenant farmers and crofters, who were only interested in the sheep, fostered the belief that deer were bad for sheep. Thus, both sides, from their different standpoints, joined in promoting the idea that deer and sheep competed for the hill pastures. Neither side wished to examine the question, or admit they were wrong, and so the idea has persisted as being the easiest course.

People often throw scorn on scientists for refusing to accept an idea until it has been proved or disproved by scientifically acceptable evidence. This is one of those cases where scientists have been shown to be right for, in recent years, the idea that sheep and deer compete and are not good for each other has been subjected to scientific investigation, both for its own sake and in connection with deer-farming. The idea has been disproved.

It would be a great mistake to reject the evidence which has come to light in the course of scientific investigation into deer-farming, even if, as the present writer believes, the right way to develop the potential of the Highland hills is by developing the deer as a stalking asset, rather than as a domesticated animal.

The most thorough purely scientific investigation into the ecology of the grazing habits of red deer and black-faced sheep on the hills of Scotland was carried out on a deer forest in Perthshire by Dr Iain Colquhoun over a four-year period from 1967 to 1971 (*The Grazing Ecology of Red Deer and Black-faced Sheep in Perthshire*, PhD thesis, Edinburgh University, 1970). The introduction to his lengthy treatise, setting out his methods and findings, commences:

My objectives in this thesis were to describe and compare the grazing ecology of red deer and black-faced sheep in order to define the ecological similarities and differences between the species, and so to assess the likelihood or otherwise of competition between them. These objectives stemmed from a wish to test the oft-repeated statement that deer and sheep compete.

His conclusion states (in relation to the stage of growth of the vegetation and the time at which it should be utilised):

> . . . sheep and deer grazing patterns generally appear to complement one another on pastures with a variety of vegetation. In spring and early summer sheep graze mostly grass swards, while deer graze heather. This suggests that at high overall grazing pressures sheep alone might over-graze grass swards and deer alone might over-graze heather swards. In June and July deer eat much more grass and much less heather, so increasing the grazing pressure on grass swards when it is most needed [Earlier he had pointed out that grass needs to be eaten just before it flowers, otherwise the strength of the plant goes into producing seed, so that grazing just before flowering produces more leaf vegetation for further grazing] and reducing pressures on heather swards just when they are thought to be most susceptible to heavy grazing. In autumn deer use less grass and more heather, and so reduce pressure on grass swards. This pattern of utilisation means that all the vegetation on the range should be in better condition, with greener and more vigorous herbage, than if either animal species grazed alone. Thus although there are some similarities in winter diet, e.g. in the intake of heather and some grass species, we can expect range carrying capacity to be higher under both species, because of the improvement in range conditions.

In other words, one species will improve the pasture for the other, and the species do not compete, as is shown by the behaviour of the one towards the other. The reader is referred to Dr Colquhoun's excellent treatise for details, which are given entirely objectively and very thoroughly.

Similar conclusions are also reached in the various scientific investigations into deer-farming; but, in most cases, they are only investigations into one or two aspects of the matter and, therefore, have to be taken together, bits from this and bits from that to get an overall picture. It is not the object of this book, still less this chapter, to analyse the scientific evidence in detail, but merely to present, in readable form, the conclusions to which the scientists have come.

That is not the end of the matter, although it might well be, because stalkers can observe for themselves many pointers to these conclusions when they are on the hill. There are many points of interest bearing on the matter, which can be checked by straightforward observation, while one is stalking.

Both sheep and deer live on the herbage of the hill, but this is very mixed, and both species are highly selective in what they eat. This point was brought home to me very forcibly when 12 red deer escaped from a park and took up residence in an adjoining barley field. Fortunately, this field had been part of the park at an earlier date, and in the middle of it was a raised clump of trees which had obviously formed part of the ornamental decoration of the park. The escape took place in early July of a very warm summer, and the deer spent each day resting in the clump of trees in the middle. They felt safe there because, as it was raised, they had a view all round, and the trees provided shade from the hot sun which, strangely enough, shone most of that summer. They escaped from the park because of contractors working there, which frightened them a lot and, although considerable effort was put into trying to drive them back from the barley field into the park, in which I assisted, this effort proved utterly futile, and they always broke back through the line of beaters until, at last, we felt we were doing more harm to the barley trying to drive the deer out than they were doing in the barley.

When the barley was cut, some two months after the deer had first taken up residence there, I enquired of the farmer how much damage had, in fact, been done, and was extremely surprised to hear that this field had given the best yield of barley, and had been far and away his cleanest crop, because the deer had eaten all the weeds growing among the corn. They had done no damage to the standing corn because of their very small legs and feet. It is true that they would have done a great deal of damage if they had lain down in the corn, but they always retreated to their wooded knoll in the middle before lying down. I do not advocate that every farmer should keep deer in his cornfield, but it does illustrate very forcibly the selective nature of their grazing. I told this story subsequently to a New Forest farmer, whose fields were subject to invasion by deer from the Forest, and he expressed no surprise.

On the hill, the habits of deer and sheep are different. Deer, as we have seen, move a good deal, and tend to fan out and feed separately, moving as they feed. Also, they tend to feed and move at night more than by day. Sheep, on the other hand, tend to stay in one place: they are what the hill sheep farmer calls 'hefted' to one place. They graze around the one place, and tend to spend the night lying on a particular dry knoll, feeding during the daytime.

If one finds a particularly wild lot of sheep when one is out stalking one day, it will be the same lot in the same place next time one stalks there: and, indeed, on my forest, I am getting to know, in the course of time, which sheep will run and which will not when they see me stalking. However, I do not recommend, except as a necessity, that stalkers should try and learn this and stalk close to sheep he thinks are tame, because that may not apply that particular day!

In general, under any particular weather conditions, the deer tend to graze higher than the sheep in the daytime, coming down through the sheep in the evening and returning again in the morning. The different grazing habits of the two species are reflected in their instinctive reaction to predators. Sheep tend to bunch up, the stronger members facing the predator from the outside, while deer use their speed to run away from predators.

This difference in grazing habits is bound to result in a difference in the actual grazing, and this is further accentuated when one remembers that sheep are pure grazers, while deer are browsers and grazers: they, therefore, use their mouths, although basically the same structure, in a different way. Sheep tend to pull the herbage off, while deer cut it off, more like the popular 'roll cut' gardening secateurs: it would be no use pulling at a supple branch! It has to be actually cut.

Incidentally, the habit of sheep in resorting to the same dry knoll in small groups every night is one of the limiting factors in the number of sheep which can be put on a hill, because it results in a rapid build-up of parasites.

I have often been asked what is the gland which stags have below and to the front of each eye: sheep do not have it, and it is another indication that deer are woodland browsers by nature. It secretes a waxy substance which the stags deposit on the end of thin branches to mark their territory. How they do it without spiking their eyes is another matter, for they get the end of the thin branch right into the hole. I suspect they also deposit some on the heather when thrashing about in the well-known fashion during the rut. A dog, when stalking, soon gets to indicate if there is a stag in the herd

Modern scientific research into deer-farming has exploded one of the dogmas which used to be very firmly held by sheep farmers, and was used to drive a wedge between sheep and deer interests; namely, that because ticks are found on deer, deer are agents in the distribution of louping ill, which is the cause of many sheep losses. However, the North of Scotland College of Agriculture bulletin of May 1978 on red deer farming states categorically that deer are not susceptible to tick-borne diseases; while the Department of Agriculture and Fisheries for Scotland 1974 Report on the Rowett Research Experimental Deer Farm states that the antibody to louping-ill virus is found in deer, but the illness has never been reported, although easily identifiable even by amateur stalkers.

The disease itself affects the brain, producing a louping gait, or a form of staggering, thus the colloquial name of 'trembling', from which the animal suffers before total paralysis sets in.

Ticks have a complicated life cycle, extending to three years, including the egg stage. They feed only for two short periods, one in the beginning of the second year, when they are in the larval stage, and the other in the third year, when they are fattening-up to produce their eggs. In both cases, they gorge themselves on the blood of the host animal, and then drop off into the mat of dead herbage on the hill. In the first case, they then pupate, and in the second, lay their eggs. Virtually the whole of the life of the tick (including the egg stage) is thus spent in the dead herbage—mostly the dead, poor quality deer grass—which must be moist. If this dead herbage is absent, the tick cannot survive. It is, therefore, important to have the hill properly grazed, so as to avoid too much dead herbage remaining throughout the year. Deer eat the dead grass during the winter, as we have already seen, so destroying the tick habitat and benefiting the sheep accordingly. Heather does not give rise to mat for ticks to live in, or provides very little at worst.

By harbouring louping ill sheep also make it available to the grouse. Grouse are one of the few native creatures which are susceptible to louping ill, nearly all the others having the necessary antibodies in their make-up. The Grouse Research Organisation has been carrying out a long research into grouse, since they, as well as deer, are of great value to the Highland economy. It has now definitely established, and published the conclusion, that the almost total extinction of grouse on the west coast of Scotland, and decrease elsewhere, is entirely due to louping ill, passed on from the sheep by ticks.

From the Nature Conservancy Research island of Rhum, off the west coast, sheep were eliminated ten or twelve years ago in order to see what the effects on the deer would be and, as a result of that, although ticks are still present, louping ill is now entirely absent. It is to be hoped that they will now try and reintroduce grouse, and see how they do, Rhum being too far from any sufficient concentration of grouse to be re-stocked naturally.

Another interesting result of the removal of sheep from Rhum is that, in many places, the herbage which the sheep normally eat has grown far too rank, and is swamping much other valuable herbage more favoured by the deer. The result is to decrease, and not increase, the food available to the deer; at least that was the case when I was last there about six years ago, and it was obvious for anybody to see.

Turning now to the economics of the position, in calculating the carrying capacity of the forest, one may allow approximately three sheep to two deer; but one should remember that the hoggs (ewe lambs) are sent away for wintering, so are not on the hill, and one must also remember that, in the spring, the ewes which are lambing should be kept down on the low ground, so that their lambing can be supervised. If they lamb up on the hill (which has been a practice in some forests, and arose when lambs were of very little value), there are bound to be cases of difficult lambing which result in the death of the lamb and/or ewe.

Deer also make much better use of the available food than sheep: the conversion ratio, that is to say, the amount of fodder required for each pound of weight put on by the animal eating the fodder, is about three times better in deer than it is in sheep. This, in spite of the fact that the fodder eaten by deer in the winter consists in a large proportion of poor quality dead grass.

When we come to the final product, namely the meat, the scales are again loaded in favour of the deer. Firstly, the deer meat (venison) is virtually all lean meat, whereas on the sheep there is a great deal of fat in the carcass weight; and secondly, deer are very light-boned creatures, for rapid running over the hills, and the proportion of carcass weight which is bone is substantially less in deer than it is in sheep. These two factors make the proportion of usable lean meat substantially higher in deer carcasses than in sheep.

It is impossible to compare usefully the prices of venison and mutton, because the former varies so much from year to year according to the continental demand. In the recent past, venison was despised and found no ready sale in Britain, but it is now becoming a fashionable meat in restaurants, commanding a high price. In Germany, last year, it was selling at a price equivalent to more than £4 per pound (0·45kg) weight. Unless there is a marked reversal in this trend, the price of venison will remain well above that of mutton, anyhow.

Dr John M. Bryden, writing in the *Journal of Agricultural Economics*, Vol XXIX No 1 January 1978, on the subject of 'Deer versus Sheep', says that there is a growing body of evidence that deer are substantially more efficient than sheep in converting hill grazings into usable meat, and that deer might well be capable of producing twice as much per hectare (2·5 acres) as sheep. Dr Bryden is, of course, the Highlands and Islands Board expert on these matters. His comparison is made in the context of deer- and sheep-farming, but it is equally true of deer on the open hill, and so will apply just the same when the deer are stalked.

Attention has already been called to the amount of foreign currency which venison produces for the country but, as this is so important at the present time, it should never be lost sight of.

The conclusion, therefore, is that, from the point of view of conservation of nature, national economics, employment, meat production, tourism and recreation, deer are more advantageous than sheep while, from the agricultural point of view, the best use of the hill grazing is obtained by joint use by deer and sheep. Thus, both should graze the hill but, if either has to go, it should be the sheep.

5
CULLING AND SEX RATIO

Having decided, in accordance with the principles mentioned before, how many deer the forest will carry, it is then necessary to build up the stock of deer to this amount, and endeavour to maintain it at that number. Deer forests are not isolated units, and deer move a good deal so that, really, the proper way of dealing with this problem is for a number of adjoining forest owners to get together and try and work out an overall policy for the largest area possible. Even then, there will be weather conditions when the bulk of the deer are found in one part of the area and other weather conditions when they are found in another, so that it will seldom be that any particular forest has exactly the planned number of deer. However, until one can work out a theoretical basis, no planning can be done.

Therefore, in this chapter, let us consider that the number of deer which the forest will adequately support is 300 adult animals, and ignore calves under a year old. Because the figures are not precise, this will make little difference but, if it is thought that the fact that there must be calves under a year old does make any material difference, then some allowance can be made in the end on a rule-of-thumb basis, but it complicates the calculations considerably to bring them in, in the first instance.

A young stag and hind (September)

For all practical purposes, one can say that deer produce one calf only when they calve: roe deer often produce twins, but we are here considering red deer. There is a recorded instance of a hind on Rhum, which is the experimental deer forest run by the Nature Conservancy, producing twins a few years ago, which, because of the rarity, received a good deal of publicity, but that has no real bearing on hill conditions because they were born at the end of September and, undoubtedly, both of them would have died in the winter under hill conditions. In addition, both parents had been heavily stimulated by the application, either by way of injection or in food, of artificial hormones, which they would not get under hill conditions. Twin calves are rarely reported in the stalking season, and I know of only one instance when these have quite definitely been identified as having been born to one hind. On the other hand, I know of quite a few instances of hinds adopting a calf, and I think that most of these reported cases of a hind being seen with two calves are cases of adoption, either temporary or permanent.

One thing most authorities seem to be agreed on is that, under normal hill conditions, the herd of hinds will produce about a third of their number in calves reaching one year old. This means that the herds increase by one third of the total hind stock each year. That does not mean one third of the total stock of course, because the total stock will also include stags.

For some reason, which has never been explained, but which is an undoubted fact, slightly more hinds are born than stags. Different authorities put the excess of hinds at different figures, but somewhere between 4% and 8% so that, if one takes 6%, one clearly will not be far wrong.

Every farmer knows that, for gregarious animals, one male for ten to twenty females, or even more, is quite enough. Sheep farmers on the hill usually work to about one ram to fifteen ewes. Why, therefore, does nature provide that stags and hinds are born in so nearly equal numbers? The answer to this is to be found in the process of evolution and survival of the fittest. Nature is very often wasteful to ensure that only the strongest males breed and it does this, in the case of deer, by allowing the cull by predators (when there were such) to be taken predominantly from the males.

Starting at the rutting season, the first thing that happens is that the knobbers, or yearling beasts, are chased out of the hind herds by the incoming stags. These young beasts have never had to fend for themselves before, and they either hang about the outside of the herds trying to get back, and not attending to their own safety (which they have never had to look after) or else they go off, perhaps two together, wandering about on their own. Every stalker will have encountered them at quite close quarters, and noticed how utterly unprepared and unaccustomed they are to looking after themselves. In either case (and probably they do first one and then the other normally), it was these young males which formed the exclusive prey of the predators in the autumn. As winter comes on, the surviving knobbers are still left wandering about on their own, though they do then begin to collect up with other stags, or even re-join the hind herds. The stags which have been rutting have run down very much, and go off, often on their own, to recover. The older the stag, the more likely it is to become solitary at this time of year. This picture continues more or less through the winter, stags tending to gather more into herds as the winter progresses into spring but, again, it is the solitary animals which would have formed the basic prey of the predators, and these are all males still. In spring, the stags lose their horns, a process which seems to worry them quite a bit, and they are still not in good condition, having put on little during the winter after the rut. They would still have formed the bulk of the predators' prey until the hinds got heavy in calf about May, when the in-calf hinds would take over. The calves are born in early June and, from then until the rut in late September, formed the staple diet of the predators.

Thus, in the truly natural state when there were predators, we have the picture of the stags of one sort or another forming their basic prey from late September until the end of April, seven months; the in-calf hinds, a month and a half; and the calves, the remaining three and a half months, when, since they are born male and female in nearly equal numbers, the toll is approximately equal. The net result, therefore, over the year, is that the stags were taken by the predators in much larger numbers than the hinds. In fact, one might say that the ratio was something like 7 to $1\frac{1}{2}$ for the eight-and-a-half-month period mentioned above, and then equally for the remaining three-and-a-half months.

This, of course, explains why they are born in nearly equal numbers.

We revert now to our supposition that the ground will support 300 adult animals, on average, throughout the year. With a ratio of stags to hinds of 1 to 1, there would be 150 hinds, which would produce 50 beasts one year old each year. To keep the herd static, one would have to cull that number, less any allowance for mortality and poaching. Each forest will have to make its own allowance for poaching, though that will not be taken into account in our calculations here; and, if a proper selection of deer is made when culling, as indicated later on, the mortality should be very small, because all animals which are likely to die should have been shot. Incidentally, from the animal's point of view, how much better it must be to have a quick clean shot than to die a lingering death of slow starvation, brought on usually by the absence of front teeth in old age, which is the usual cause of death.

If one maintains a ratio of stags to hinds of 1 to 3, then there will be 225 hinds, which will produce 75 beasts to one year old each year and, again, subject to the above allowances made for each particular place, that will be the appropriate number to cull each year. In other words, if one has to cull 50 beasts each year, it will be about 24 stags and 26 hinds, and if one has to cull 75 each year it will be 36 stags and 39 hinds. These two figures of stag culls are set out as the annual cull in Tables 1 and 2 below but, before considering these tables, it is necessary to consider how many stags we require for breeding purposes.

A stag can conveniently cover 10 hinds, at least, in a breeding season. It is desirable that some of the younger stags should breed, but stags should not breed for too long, otherwise they will be breeding from their own offspring, as the tendency is to return to the same breeding ground each year. A happy medium may be achieved by allowing one stag in the age-group 6 to 11 years per 10 hinds for breeding purposes. Thus, for 150 hinds, 15 stags in this age-group are required; while, for 225 hinds, 22 stags in this age-group are required. Provided there is a sufficiency of stags between 6 and 11 years (which is the mature age-group) the stags under 6 years will not be allowed to breed by the older stags, or more or less so.

TABLE 1

Year of age	No before cull	Annual cull	Stock after cull	
13	2	2	—	
12	2	—	2	⎫
11	4	2	2	⎪
10	4	—	4	⎬ 22 breeding stags
9	5	1	4	⎪
8	5	—	5	⎭
7	5	—	5	
6	5	—	5	Breeding reserve
5	6	1	5	⎫
4	12	6	6	⎪ Culls for venison
3	25	13	12	⎬
2	36	11	25	⎭
TOTALS		36	75	

Stags should, in theory, be shot before they rut, and the number calculated after the cull. It might be argued that stags would breed satisfactorily after they are 12, but they reach their prime at about 12, and after that are going back. Also, they would probably be breeding with their own young, as mentioned above, so that,

49

ideally, all stags should be shot at 13 or before. That is, of course, only theory and some will undoubtedly escape. On the hill, they might live until they are 15: park stags have reached 20 or even more.

Using the above as a theoretical basis, the pattern of cull on a 1 to 3 ratio works out as shown in Table 1. This gives an annual cull of 31 stags, used purely for venison (which will be better as the stags are shot young, although the weight may be slightly less than if they were shot older), 1 in middle age, which allows for some mistake, and 4 'trophy' heads shot in their prime, which also produce a good weight of venison. This allows 22 breeding stags between the ages of 6 and 12, which is enough for 225 hinds.

TABLE 2

Year of age	No. before cull	Annual cull	Stock after cull	
13	3	3	—	
12	5	2	3	
11	7	2	5	
10	9	2	7	50 breeding stags
9	12	3	9	
8	14	2	12	
7	16	2	14	
6	18	2	16	
5	20	2	18	
4	22	2	20	Culls for venison
3	24	2	22	
2	24	—	24	
TOTALS		24	150	

Table 2 sets out the position which would arise if the continental system were followed of maintaining a ratio of 1 stag to 1 hind, and shooting the same number of stags from each age-group, as far as possible, on the basis of the 'Hoffman Pyramid' favoured on the Continent. Here it will be seen that there are far more than the necessary number of breeding stags in the age bracket 6 to 12 years for 150 hinds. It will produce more 'trophy' heads, provided all the mature stags remain on the ground to be shot, but this is a very big proviso with so many mature stags, and it is much more likely that some of the good stags, which have been carefully preserved, will go off to neighbouring forests and get shot there. The average weight of stag, and therefore the average amount of venison per stag, will be more because, generally, the stags are shot older; but the total amount of venison produced will be very much down as compared with Table 1, simply because 50% less stags will have been shot.

The net result, therefore, of these two systems will be that maintaining a 1 to 3 ratio will give 50% more stalks or, at least, stags to be shot; more and better quality venison (probably about 35% more because the main increase of weight and growth occurs in the early years, followed by a much more gradual increase); and, say 5 good heads, being the stags shot between 9 and 13. Conversely, of course, there will be twice as many 'trophy' heads on the 1 to 1 basis, but there will be 50% less stalking and less venison.

When one takes into account the hind cull as well (which should be taken on the old hinds on either basis) the 3 to 1 ratio, where 39 hinds are shot each year, will yield 50% more hind venison than the 1 to 1 ratio basis, where only 26 hinds are shot each year.

Many people will think that the 1 stag to 3 hinds basis will produce quite enough 'trophy' stag heads; and these stags will have been left after much more careful selection of the poor heads at younger age, so that, on the whole, they should be better. It may also be thought that this is enough 'trophy' heads for the number of deer (300) which is being considered: otherwise, a 'trophy' head ceases to be, in fact, just that and becomes too commonplace.

In the following chapter, we shall consider the selection of stags to be shot, but every practical stalker will, of course, be saying that the selection of bad heads at a young age, particularly the selection of bad knobbers, is very difficult. It is appreciated that this is so, but it does add quite a lot to the challenge of stalking, and so to its enjoyment, on the one hand and, on the other hand, the cull set out in Table 1 is the theory for the best cull. Until one knows the theory, it is useless to start on any planned operations.

The (false) desire for quality heads has been the reason why many forests in Scotland have endeavoured to shoot on a 1 to 1 basis, and many other people have advocated a 1 to 1 basis on the ground that the more stags you have, the more you can shoot. It sounds so nice and easy, but it is clearly wrong, when one considers the matter in any detail at all, for the simple reason that it is the hinds which produce the young to form the additions to the herds each year.

It will be noticed that the old rule-of-thumb idea that the correct

Young stags: one with a horn broken, the result of a fight or damage when in velvet (probably the latter, because of the kink); in either case, next year's horns will be all right

cull is approximately one sixth of the total stock is not far off, when one takes into account poaching and a certain number of kills by farmers on enclosed land, but the theoretical cull should be based on the annual recruitment to the stock and not on an overall figure of total stock of both sexes.

Other tables for other sex ratios can be worked out and, where the ratio is even higher, a larger number of stags can be killed. However, most of these have to be killed young and there is a danger, therefore, that too few will be left for the stalking season, so that, on balance, a 1 to 3 ratio is the happy solution to a complex problem, in practice.

Too many mature rutting stags are not a good thing, because they tend to fight too much, and expend too much of their energy on that rather than the correct job in hand! It also results in their being too run-down to winter satisfactorily. Too few are also a disadvantage from the stalking point of view because some are, in fact, required for shooting during the rut; and also, although a stag will cover more than 10 hinds quite happily, there is again a tendency to get too run-down for the winter, and the young stags, which are of unknown quality, will, in practice, get in and rut.

It has to be borne in mind that the rut must last about three weeks at least, because hinds come into season once in 20 days and only for a few hours. Three weeks is longer than any stag can hold a herd of hinds against all comers without getting too run-down to winter under hill conditions so that, in practice, some of the younger stags will rut.

6

RECOGNITION OF TYPE OF DEER

As we have already seen, in the state in which nature intended deer
to be, the larger predators took a substantial cull of the deer, and it is
this cull which now has to be taken by man, in order to preserve the
deer herds at their proper numbers and in proper health. The latter
aspect should not be lost sight of, because the removal of unhealthy
stock helps to preserve the general health of the whole herd,
although it is true that deer suffer from very few diseases, and seem
able to cope with most of the common forms of parasite. No doubt,
this is due to the culling of the unhealthy beasts by the predators in
days gone by.

Predators took the old, the young, the solitary, the weak and the
unhealthy: man can do better than this, because his basis of selection
of those to be culled can be made purely with an eye to the improvement of the herds. Predators were merely in search of food and took
the easiest: this did include the unhealthy and the old but, when
man does it, he need not take the very young or necessarily the
solitary, and he can select the bad heads.

A proper culling policy, therefore, is dependent upon recognition
of the right deer to cull and this, in turn depends, to a large extent,
on being able to assess correctly on the hill the age of deer. This

An old hind (foreground) with a young hind

will be done through a telescope or binoculars before the shot, but it is as well to check the assessment of the age made *before* the shot by ascertaining it accurately *after* the deer has been killed, so as to verify the correctness of the judgement made in the first instance.

The checking of age after the deer is dead is comparatively easy, by checking the wear on the teeth. Deer chew the cud with a sort of round action and, consequently, the molars wear down. The calves and yearlings are easy to distinguish, anyhow, so that it is not necessary to go into the question of milk teeth or when the full mouth is obtained but, once it has grown, there is a sharp, saw-like effect on the inside edge of the molars. This wears down gradually until, by the age of about 12 or 13, the first molar will be almost flat. There are 3 molars behind the pre-molars, and these are the ones to look at. Very often (but not invariably), the third molar has a little extra bit at the back and there will be a semi-circular indentation in this into which a pencil point can be inserted when the molar is first grown. As it wears down, this indentation disappears until, by the age of about 10, it will have disappeared altogether, and only a brown patch of dentine remains: this is an easy small point to look for. Ageing by teeth is professionally done by cutting a section of the tooth and examining it under a microscope, when rings corresponding to each year's growth can be seen, very much the same as the rings on a tree. However, most people will not wish to do this, or may not feel competent to do it, although it is not difficult. The difficulty really arises in fairly old stags, where the first ring becomes indistinct and there is sometimes doubt about where to start counting.

The easy way out is to get a board and keep half of the lower jaw of deer of various ages on it, with the ages marked, then a ready comparison can be made. The original board is best made by comparison with another board, or by sending lower jaws to one of the universities and asking for some of the teeth to be ring-counted. That will fix at least some of them and, providing they are selected with care, showing little or a good deal of wear and so on, a board can easily be made up. It is better to have a board made up for one's own forest because the deer may, on that particular forest, eat more heather and less grass or vice versa, and wear at some forests is slightly more than at others, in consequence.

Turning now to the more complicated but much more important point of recognition on the hill, the first thing to look at is the head. As with humans, and nearly everything else, the head seems to go on growing with age on the whole though, of course, the head will also be proportionate to the size of the animal. In a stag, the head appears to widen out more, which is no doubt to carry the larger horns which normally increase in size and weight each year. Hinds' heads, on the other hand, tend to lengthen rather than broaden out. In fact a stag's head also lengthens, but the effect of the broadening is to disguise the longer appearance. The ears also seem to grow, though do not be misled by the fact that a yearling appears to have very long ears simply because it has a small head. Thus, an old hind will have an almost pointed look to her nose and definitely long, and often untidy, ears.

The carriage of the head is also very important: just as humans tend to stoop with age, so a deer, as it gets older, carries its head lower. Looking at a deer when it is either walking quietly or standing looking about, it will be apparent that a young deer will carry the head high, with a very distinct curve of the neck from the shoulders onwards, while an old beast will carry the head lower, the bottom of the neck and shoulders being almost in a straight line and only the top half of the neck curving upwards. For this recognition sign to be valid, deer must be at ease; even an old hind can stretch her neck straight upwards when she is alarmed and looking about; and all deer can put their heads down to graze.

As a stag gets older, its neck thickens, which must not be confused with the ruffling out of the fur which occurs in the rut, and allowance must be made for this ruffling out, which is often referred to as thickening of the neck. The result of this thickening of the neck, and the fact that the neck sticks out from the shoulder in a horizontal line parallel to the top of the back, tends to make older stags look as if they have a shorter neck than young stags, though this is not, in fact, so. With the lower carriage of the neck, the top of the withers tends to stick up, and this gets more pronounced in stags than hinds; thus, in an old stag, there will be a line along the top of the back, then a definite hump above the shoulders, and then a continuation of the line of the back at the base of the neck until it begins to curve up fairly near the head.

A young beast of either sort will have well-defined features, sharp and clean cut. There is usually a black line of hair running down the middle of the face which is well defined in young beasts, but loses its definition as the deer gets older. The skin of the face is tight and neat in a young beast but then, in middle age, the appearance of tightness seems to go, to reappear in old age; but, in this stage, the veins often stand out, whereas they do not in the young beast. Greyness of the hairs of the face and muzzle is an indication of age, but it is often not very pronounced, or does not occur at all. It is, therefore, only a thing to look for as a confirmation of other points, rather than as a criterion in itself.

The condition of the coat is always important, and incomplete or late moults, or a generally bad coat, are indications either of age or ill-health.

So far, the indications which we have considered apply to stags and hinds, but a stag's antlers are also very indicative. However, since we may wish to cull stags because of the quality of the antlers alone, what to look for in the antlers is considered separately below.

When hind-shooting, it is always as well to remember that the herd will be led by an old hind. It may be that a younger hind sees

Good young stag with (below) a young hind and an old hind

the stalking party first and starts to go off, but she will always slow down and wait for the leading hind, which will be an old hind, to lead the herd on in whatever she considers to be the safest direction, so that, once they have really started moving, the herd will always be led by the oldest hind, or one of the oldest hinds. Similarly, if they have become nervous and are just milling around, as they sometimes do, it will be an old hind who finally leads off. Therefore, if in doubt or in a hurry when out hind-shooting, it is safe to shoot the leading hind. This, incidentally, will have the effect of stopping the herd and, if one is trying to catch up on numbers (as so often happens hind-shooting), a second can then be taken.

We have referred to old and young, and it should be remembered that, under Highland conditions, a hind is old at 10 or 11 and a stag at 12 to 14.

When spying a herd before shooting, which should always be done at leisure and at length, except in exceptional circumstances, indications of weaklings, or ill or injured deer, should always be looked for. Injuries are many and different, so that no useful purpose can be achieved by describing any particular injury in detail, but the stalker should get used to the normal movement of deer, so that any which move stiffly or differently will at once be noticed. Animals do lie in all sorts of different positions, but one lying very awkwardly should be examined with care through the telescope and, if it moves and is healthy, it will move normally and will lie down in a much more normal position whereas, if there is something wrong with it, it will move awkwardly and probably lie down again in an awkward-looking position. The appearance of the coat is also very indicative of the condition of the deer, as has already been noted. Apart from stags in the rut, a very pinched appearance of the stomach, similar to a run stag, almost certainly means the deer is off its food.

Those which are very ill or wounded tend to go off on their own for solitude, but that is only in the later stages. In the case of stags, some conditions may be reflected in their antlers and, in particular, injury to the genital organs always shows itself in malformation of the horns. The peruke-type head, which is rare in red deer, results from this injury or non-development of those organs, and I have one head from a ten-year-old stag which had clearly never developed in this respect, and grew only short, thick horns which clearly never cast their velvet at all and, indeed, I doubt if the horn had ever been cast. On the whole, deer seem to be able to cope with liver-fluke, even on ground infested with this parasite but, where stags do get a bad parasitic infestation of the liver, this nearly always shows itself in the horn, in a corkscrew effect.

Let us now turn to the types of head which should be shot. First of all, there are the obvious ones, such as the switch, or head with either no points at all, or simply brow points and then nothing. Beyond looking ugly, they are a danger to other stags when fighting, because the absence of tines high up make the main horn more likely to penetrate another stag and so wound it. Stags when fighting, and this, of course, goes for switches as well, first of all walk side by side, evidently each trying to size the other up. If this does not result in one stag deciding that he is the weaker and going off, they then put their heads down in a pushing match. This usually does not result in injury but, when they break off, one stag may give the other a jab in the side as it turns off, and this is where the switch does injury to other stags. Knobbers or second-year stags, of course, have no points, and a good knobber, which, not infrequently, gets quite a substantial neck in the rutting season, should not be shot as a switch. After a bad winter, a third-year stag may also still look very like a knobber but, in that case, it will probably never make much and can be shot. There are also stags which have very long, single, top points and, perhaps, three below; these are half way to switches and should be shot for the same reason. Secondly, hummels (hornless stags) or one-horned stags should also be shot: they will almost certainly breed true to type. In the case of one-horned stags, it may be that the pedicle or piece of bone on which the horn grows has been damaged in fighting and, in that case, it would not pass on the tendency to be one-horned to its offspring, but this is not a thing that one is likely to be able to spot through a telescope before the stag is shot, so one-horned stags, whatever the cause, should be shot.

Thirdly, ill-balanced heads should be shot, unless the ill-balance is due to damage of one horn in velvet. Stags not infrequently catch their horns either on a branch or a wire fence while they are soft and in velvet and, in that case, the horn may bend or even stop growing but a bend, or at least a lump, can always be seen after the horn has cleaned and, if the imbalance is due to that alone, then that stag can be left, as it will not pass on any tendency to malformation, and will grow a good head next year as long as the coronet and pedicle are not damaged.

Those, then, should be weeded out but it will be necessary to shoot more. What, therefore, are the characteristics to look for in heads which will ultimately develop into good heads? A young stag in its third, fourth or fifth year which is going to develop into a good head will not necessarily have a long horn, but it will have plenty of small, even points, and the horns will be well balanced, one corresponding almost exactly with the other. It will not at this age, however, have developed its proper shape. Many good young stags are shot because they are said to be narrow, but the span does not become apparent until, probably, the sixth year.

The shape is very important: there are two main shapes, one being the barrel shape, where the horns form almost a circle, the topmost points coming fairly close together in the middle, and the other, the wide shape, where the bottom part of the main horn goes fairly straight out at about $45°$ from the vertical when looked at from the front, and then turns upwards and slightly inwards towards the top, but the topmost points are still well apart. It is a pure matter of choice which of these two heads is preferred: both look very nice. The latter usually gives a better span, that is to say, the maximum distance between the insides of the two main horns and, therefore, may have a slight edge on the barrel shape in calculating the points value of the head on the continental points system but, apart from that, there is nothing much except choice between the two types of head. In either case, there must be a good span and a good spread, the latter being the maximum distance between the outside part, whatever it is, of the two horns: it is usually the tips of the trez, or third point up.

Again, on the continental points scale, the number of points is one of the weighting factors; but, for a wild Scottish head, from the point of view of pure beauty, a royal or twelve-point stag is probably as good as anything and, probably, the maximum which can reasonably be obtained with full development of the points under Highland conditions, except by substantial feeding. For the purists, a true royal has a cup, that is to say, three points on top forming a sort of cup which would hold a tennis ball or some similar object, and not three points in line, but I can see no great merit in this distinction, which is indeed now being dropped, to a large extent. There is some basis for saying that the true wild head does not have double brows and develops three on top before developing the bez or second tine. I do not know whether there is anything in this but, certainly, some wild heads do develop the cup on top and do look very fine without any double brows.

Summing up, therefore, after the age of about six, a good head must have developed a good shape and must, over the next three years at least, develop a good beam, that is to say a good thickness of horn, with well-developed points, gradually getting longer each year over this period. The head will remain much the same, probably, under Highland conditions, from ten to twelve, that is to say, it will be in its prime then, as will the stag and, after that, it will probably start to go back. The word 'probably' is used because it will depend to a certain amount on the grazing and the stamina of the particular stag but, by fourteen at any rate, it will be going back and, under adverse conditions, with a stag of no great stamina, it may start to go back after ten.

The indications of a stag going back are the presence of knobs or small excrescences, even amounting to small points (the old stalker's definition of a point being anything on which a ring can be hung). These are usually indications that there has been a point in previous years at that position, coupled with a shortening and deterioration of the horn. A stag in its prime usually has a good, rough, dark-coloured horn, while an old stag, and often a young one, has a whitish horn: that is not an invariable criterion, but is an indication. The horn emerges white when it cleans from velvet, and the dark colour is mainly due to rolling in the peat: the rough horn retains the dirt and peat better than the smoother horn of the old stag.

Old stags should be shot once they show any sign of going back, not because they will do any harm to the stock but because, as has been mentioned elsewhere, the process of dying from old age on the hill is a long and painful one, and a quick clean shot must be much more humane, especially when this is coupled with the fact that it is necessary to shoot the required number of stags to keep the herds in good condition in the absence of predators.

7
STALKING EQUIPMENT

Those who are familiar with the Scottish hills will not find much new to them in this chapter, which is designed for those who have stalked in other parts of the world, or are unfamiliar with the terrain. It is most important to be adequately equipped for Highland stalking and, also, to know what is involved, since otherwise the enjoyment will be greatly reduced, if not absent altogether; and furthermore the unprepared person is a nuisance to others accompanying him, and may indeed be a danger to himself.

The Highland hills are bleak, exposed places, and although there is very little ground over 4000ft (1200m), and not a great deal over 3000ft (900m), there can be a great deal of difference between the top of the hill and the sheltered valley where the lodge will almost certainly be situated; and there can be rapid changes of weather during the day.

In recent years, hill transport in the form of tracked vehicles and multi-wheeled, low-pressure-tyred vehicles has come into use. In addition to that, with the advent of excavators and allied equipment, it has been possible to make hill roads suitable for Land Rovers part of the way up the hills. Whereas, 25 years ago, it would have been necessary for anybody undertaking stalking in the Highlands to be

Bringing the stag home

fit enough to walk 15 miles (25km) in the day up quite steep hills and over rough ground, this distance can now be reduced by the use of such hill transport. Even so, nobody (without detailed knowledge of the particular forest) should really attempt it, unless he is fit enough to walk at least 5 or 10 miles (10 or 15km) over the hill. If there is any doubt about his walking capacity, he should satisfy himself that hill transport is available on the forest where he proposes to stalk.

Of course, it has always been possible to hire a pony to ride but, even then, during the actual stalk, which may involve quite a considerable amount of walking, the pony has to be left behind, and a pony-man has to be provided to look after it. He may be the same pony-man who looks after the pony used to bring the stag down after it has been shot. In that case, two ponies will be required, if the person concerned is not prepared to walk home; and, unless the ground is really handy, a pony cannot be expected to take a person out on the outward journey and a stag back on the return journey every day of the week. Those who have not tried it should also appreciate that a deer saddle is far from comfortable to ride, and a 'combination' saddle is not a great deal better. A stag cannot be put on a pony on anything except a proper deer saddle or a proper combination saddle.

As to clothing, that is bound to depend to some extent on personal taste and the weather. It can be very hot on a sunny day on the hills, even on top, and on a cold day it can be extremely cold, particularly if there is a wind. My choice, therefore, is for what I may call layer clothing, so that one can shed and put in a haversack the inner layer, if necessary. I find one of the quilted under-jackets is much the best, but the top layer must be either a khaki or olive green combat-type jacket (better still a camouflaged one) or, alternatively, a tweed jacket or something similar. A tweed jacket is probably the best from the point of view of the actual approach to the deer, but it is not nearly as wind- or rain-resistant as the modern jackets. Bright colours, of course, show up on the hill, but what people sometimes forget is that black, or near black, shows up almost as badly; khaki, medium brown or medium green is therefore much the best.

A cap or deerstalker hat is virtually essential because, when getting close in to deer, one must have one's head in sight of the deer in order to get a shot, and without a cap a forehead or, even worse, a bald head, shows up very much! If you can possibly do without it, a scarf or muffler should be avoided because, if you are doing your own stalking, it is essential to notice any change of wind, which is felt on the back or sides of the neck: after a bit, it becomes almost automatic to notice these changes as soon as they occur.

For the lower regions, any comfortable breeches or 'plus twos' will do, but they must allow full bending of the knee: many so-called walking breeches do not. The most important item, however, is a good pair of boots or shoes. Unless you are used to walking on rough ground in shoes, boots should be worn, because there is nothing more infuriating than to sprain an ankle early in a holiday; and the ground *is* rough. There are many hill boots available now which do not make the ankles sore, even if you are unused to wearing boots, but not all of them have suitable soles which really do give a good grip. Under most conditions, leather soles with proper nails give the best grip, but they are not so easy to obtain now, and they do suffer from one disadvantage, namely, that, when one is walking over rocks on a still day, they make a noise, which the deer hear on the final stages of the stalk. The other choice is the commando-type rubber sole, but that must have deep grooves in the sole, and these must be at different angles. The type of rubber sole which merely has grooves across the sole, or cleats running across it, is not suitable for traversing or walking along the side of a hill, because one simply slips down the slope: there are other soles where the grooves are not deep enough to get a good grip. The disadvantage of rubber is that water, to some extent, lubricates it, and, therefore, when crossing smooth stones, in a burn for instance, special care has to be taken when wearing rubber soles of any sort. Water does not lubricate leather soles and therefore they do not suffer from this disadvantage. Equally rubber slips on ice very much more than studded leather soles do. It is important not to slip and fall down, not only for one's own safety but, also, so as not to damage telescopes, binoculars or telescopic sights on rifles which one may be carrying.

Finally, it can be very wet on the hill, but there are many good short waterproofs and over-trousers available, the latter being particularly useful where one has to crawl or sit on wet ground during a stalk. However, the waterproof coat must be of an oiled material. The trousers may be of that, or a darkish green or grey plastic on fabric, but the one essential, whatever one chooses, is that it must, beyond being really waterproof, be free from rustle. Many of the nylon or similar waterproofs now available rustle even as one moves, and very much more so when one is crawling or sliding along the ground, making a noise which the deer never fail to hear on the final stage of a stalk! It is absolutely essential, therefore, when choosing a mackintosh to crumple the material together to test whether it is silent or makes a rustle. Whatever is taken should be as light as practicable, within the above limits, because it should be possible to put it in a small bag for carrying. This bag also serves a very useful purpose as a rest for the rifle when taking a shot, or to raise oneself up in an awkward position. However, it is essential to remember that, whatever one wants, one has to carry, except for any part of the time in hill transport. The coat must be short, for it is impossible to crawl in a full-length mackintosh.

The next essential item of equipment is either binoculars or telescope, or both. Personally, I always take both, for use as described later on.

There are any number of binoculars on the market now, but the average optician or camera shop which sells them either does not appreciate, or refuses to discuss, the most important feature from the point of view of stalking. Physically, there are three specifications for optical instruments such as binoculars or telescopes, namely, magnification, which is always quoted as 'X', say 8X; field of view, which is usually given as so many yards at a thousand yards; and resolving power. The first two of these are usually readily available, but it is the resolving power on which makers and shops are usually somewhat reticent: the resolving power is, roughly speaking, the clarity. If one is forced to compare various pairs of binoculars in a street, as is often the case at a shop, then, in order to check the resolving power, one should pick something like a slated roof, as far off as possible, and see which of the binoculars shows the cracks between the slates most distinctly. It will come as a great surprise to many people to find that one, say 8X, binocular will show the cracks quite sharply and distinctly, whereas, what appears superficially to be a similar pair of 8X will not. What resolving power really means is the ability to resolve the image of two thin black lines on a white surface close together into two black lines when seen at a distance through the binoculars, rather than show them as one thicker black line. This is of the utmost importance on on the hill, because it is the clarity of the image that makes all the difference, either in being able to pick out the type of head of a stag or, indeed, pick out the deer from the background, against which they are very well camouflaged. If the binoculars give a slightly blurred image and, by that, I do not mean actually fuzzy but not sharp, then, however much they magnify it, it will not become any sharper or clearer.

Generally speaking, 8X or 10X is probably the best magnification for binoculars for the hill. Once you get above this magnification, it becomes difficult to hold the binoculars steady enough without a rest, especially in the wind, and then the advantage of additional magnification is lost by the vibration or shaking. A reasonably large object glass (which is the other measurement, which is always given with binoculars in mm) is necessary because, on the hill, it will collect more light under conditions of bad light. But there, again, the quality of the glass is probably more important than the size of the object glass and, whatever one chooses, one has to strike a balance between something which is handy to carry and use, and something which is too big for these purposes.

For most purposes, a 20X telescope will be sufficient. Most of what has already been said about binoculars applies to telescopes, but it must be remembered that binoculars now are all of the prismatic type, and a certain amount of light is bound to be lost in going through the prisms, so that a telescope loses less light than a binocular, other things, such as quality of glass, being equal. A telescope 20X or above must be used with a rest to be any real use: one does not carry about a tripod, but rests the instrument on the knee, or on a rock, stick or whatever is handy. Telescopes and binoculars suffer from getting water inside them in wet weather, which clouds the lenses: there are now some waterproof binoculars, though they are very expensive. It is, however, just worth mentioning that the more draw-tubes a telescope has, the more wet tends to get inside when it is closed after use and, therefore, it is always as well to try and dry the outside of the tubes before they are closed, and to avoid using the telescope more than necessary in the rain.

A final word of warning on optical instruments: if used in the sun, the object glass flashes very much, just like a mirror, and many deer have been frightened a long way off by the stalker carelessly waving a telescope about.

So far, we have said little about the actual killing of the deer, largely because that is probably, to many, the least enjoyable part of the whole proceedings. However, it is a necessary part, both to control the size of the herd and to keep the deer wild, for deer become tame, and bold to enter farming ground, very readily unless they are stalked and shot.

The essential thing is that the shot should produce a clean, quick kill. What actually kills the animal is the shock more than anything else. The shock depends, of course, on where the animal is hit but, apart from that, it depends on the amount of energy transmitted to the animal from the bullet. The amount of energy which the bullet has is a direct product (multiplication) of the weight of the bullet and the velocity at the point of impact. The whole of the energy is absorbed if the bullet does not pass through the animal but, if it does pass through, a certain amount of the energy will go on in the bullet as it emerges at the other side.

Modern expanding bullets are therefore designed to expand on impact, and deliver the whole of the shock to the animal: they also break up in doing this, and inflict more actual injury inside, so accelerating the death. Again, it is a matter of compromise: too large a bullet or bore of the rifle makes too much mess of the venison, and the rifle probably kicks too much for convenient use, or it is too heavy to carry conveniently.

In a brief survey, it is not necessary to go into the ballistics of the various types of rifle, which are better discussed in a book on ballistics or with a reputable gun-maker, when buying the rifle. Suffice it to say that the law in the British Isles is, quite rightly, that no rifle below a calibre of .240 (6·096mm) or a muzzle energy of 1700 ft lb (2300J) should be used but even this muzzle energy is too low for using on red deer and, generally speaking, anything larger than .303 (7·696mm) is too big.

The .270 (6·858mm) with a 150 grain soft-nosed bullet is probably about the ideal compromise, and is now very widely used in the Highlands. This has a muzzle velocity of 2802 ft/s (854m/s), a velocity at 200yd (180m) of 2436 ft/s (742m/s) and a striking energy at 100yd (90m) of 2280 ft lb (3090J), or 2000 ft lb (2701J) at 200yd (180m).

There is also a 130 grain bullet for the .270 'Winchester': this has a muzzle velocity of 3140 ft/s (957m/s), and a velocity of 2639 ft/s (804m/s) at 200yd (180m). The striking energy at 100yd (90m) is 2401 ft lb (3255J) and at 200yd (180m) 2011 ft lb (2727J). These are slightly better figures than those for the 150 grain bullet, but I prefer the latter because with it (a) the wear on the barrel is less, (b) any deflection by grass, etc is less and (c) on hitting bone there is less tendency to break up too soon or ricochet; but the differences are only slight, as is shown by the almost identical striking energies at 200yd (180m). For comparison, the striking energy of the .243 (6·172mm) Winchester 100 grain bullet drops to 1430 ft lb (1940J) at 200yd (180m) and the .303 Service rifle to 1569 ft lb (2119J). See page 138 for full details.

If open sights are used, the back sight should be of a shallow 'v' type, and the foresight must be small. However, eyesight must be

very good to use open sights and they are not now generally
favoured. Telescopic sights are now, therefore, in general use, and
there are many good makes available. The disadvantages of telescopic
sights over open sights are that they are not quite as quick to get on
to deer, they do suffer from getting fogged up in bad weather
(though the better the make, the less this occurs) and, finally, they
are very subject to getting knocked off centre, particularly if the
person carrying the rifle falls on it or anything like that. With care,
however, the advantages can far outweigh the disadvantages because
more accurate shooting can be achieved, they are better in a bad
light and they can be adapted to the eyesight of the shooter. The
main trouble of getting knocked off centre can be avoided with care
but, even so, it is essential to check the sight frequently. A rough
check can be made by removing the bolt and looking down the
barrel at a distant object, and then looking at it through the telescopic sight, though, if the rifle is sighted to shoot at 200yd (180m),
the image through the telescopic sight will be two or three inches
above the image down the centre of the barrel; the amount should be
known from the tables of ballistics supplied with the rifle; or there
is now an instrument available from gunmakers which fits down the
barrel and is calibrated to suit the telescopic sight.

The best magnification is probably 4X, though it is largely a
matter of choice. However, too great a magnification reduces the
field too much to find a beast quickly if necessary, and also, probably,
there is a tendency to take too long a shot. The mounting of the
telescopic sight is most important. It is a matter for the gunmaker
but it must be firm and, if the sight is demountable, it must be
checked frequently.

The type of graticule in the sight is a matter of personal preference
but, before settling on one particular type, it is essential to look at it
against something about the same size as a deer at a range of, say,
200yd (180m), because some of the graticules supplied with a single
pillar have much too wide a top to the pillar, so making accurate
shooting difficult. They are no doubt good in bad light, or for
close-range work, but that is not what is wanted in the Scottish
Highlands. My personal choice is for cross hairs.

As well as the necessity for checking the alignment of the telescopic sight at frequent intervals, and particularly at the beginning
of the season, people who go to a forest which is new to them should

remember the often quoted words of the old stalker who, on being confronted with a guest newly arrived from London, and clearly newly equipped by the most expensive London tailor and gunmaker, said 'We will now go to the target before going out', to which the guest replied vehemently that all his equipment had been tested and checked thoroughly by a well-known gunmaker, and to which, in turn, the reply was 'It's no the rifle we are testing'. A stalker's task is made much easier and more satisfactory if he knows the skill and limitations, if any, of his guests, rather than having to wonder all through the stalk, possibly after some previous unsatisfactory experience. So guests should never take it amiss if they are asked to have a shot at the target.

After a stag has been shot, the problem of getting it down off the hill arises, although a number of people would like to forget this. One cannot just put it in a game bag! Until fairly recently, the choice was either to put it on a pony or, in a few forests, on a sledge behind a pony, or else to drag it, but now there are various forms of hill transport available as well.

Dragging is still resorted to on some forests where the number of deer shot does not justify other means of transport or, as is much more common, where the other means of transport has broken down. Dragging is very hard work, especially if there is the least bit of uphill or even over any long length of level ground. Although I have dragged a large number of stags, I would never advocate it, if it is possible to avoid it, and it has probably accounted for more back injuries than any other thing. If it is attempted, it should be done by attaching a rope to the head and forefeet of the stag and putting the other end of the rope round a stick, which two people can hold, one on either side of the rope, to get a good pull.

A pony is undoubtedly the best means of getting a stag off the hill because, with the exception of very boggy ground and peat hags, a good hill pony can go practically anywhere; and, on a sentimental basis, a stag carried home on the back of a pony seems a much more fitting end for the noble beast than being dumped ignominiously in the back of some transport!

Except in unusual circumstances, it requires two men to load a pony, and a pony itself requires a pony-man to lead it. Usually nowadays, the difficulty is not so much getting a hill pony as getting a pony-man. He can follow the stalking party so far, but then has to be left behind, because a pony is too large to take on the actual stalk, and it is essential, therefore, that proper communication signals between the stalking party and the pony-man should be arranged, and the latter given absolutely clear instructions as to how long and where to wait and so on.

Waiting can be a very poor job on a cold day, which, perhaps, accounts for the difficulty in getting pony-men, but stalkers should remember how unpleasant it is, try to find shelter, and not keep pony-men waiting too long. I appreciate that is easier said than done in certain circumstances, but an endeavour should be made. I have spent many hours on the hill chasing pony-men who had not waited or had gone the wrong way at the wrong time, although the stalker had given what he considered to be clear instructions. This is nearly as irritating as having the pony appear over the skyline in the middle of a stalk!

Normally, the loading of the stag is the job of the professionals, but everyone who may stalk for himself should know how to do it.

The first thing to remember is that the horns must never touch the pony: to let them do so is a sure way of frightening it. The stag, therefore, is loaded with its back towards the pony's neck, lying slightly on its front, with the head bent round so that it sits on top of the stag with the horns uppermost.

The saddle should have four straps, one on each of the lower rings and two on the top or centre ring: but one of the latter is a spare and should only be used if one of the others breaks. The girths must be fully tightened before loading is started.

To load, get the stag on to the top of a convenient rock or bank, and the pony standing below. Some ponies will only stand if a coat is put over their heads: there is nothing wrong in that, but one should know if this is so. The stronger man should lift the front end of the stag, taking a grip which will keep the head above the body of the stag. The less strong man takes the rear end and lifts the hind legs across the saddle. He then goes quickly round to the other side of the pony and brings the strap attached to the lower ring round over the lower haunch, between the legs and under the upper haunch, and secures it to its buckle on the other lower ring of the saddle. This strap should be slack, and the stag pushed over so that it rests on it: the stag will now be well over to that side.

The first man then puts his lower strap over the lower front leg of the stag, across its chest, and then under the top front leg, leaving this strap loose (tighten later, see below). He then passes the top strap round the horn once, preferably the top horn but, depending on the size and shape, it may be the lower, and tightens it fully, pulling the head down on to the stag tightly.

The stag must now be balanced by tightening the haunch strap and pushing the stag back towards the front end until it is evenly balanced on the pony (hence the reason for leaving the front end strap fairly loose). Both straps are now tightened fully. It should be noted that the function of these straps is to keep the stag at the point of balance, but not to take the weight, except as far as necessary to keep it balanced. The top strap really only keeps the head down and back.

I once had an excellent pony that would not start at all after the stag had been put on until it had given a firm bite and tug to make sure the stag was secure and to its liking. This always confused new pony-men, who, after the stag had been loaded, tried to lead the pony off, when it simply stood still, as its head was held so that it could not bite the stag: but, once satisfied, it went home excellently.

If the amateur stalker does have to take out an inexperienced pony-man with no professional stalker, then it is essential that he gets detailed instructions on how to secure the stag, and he must know over what ground the pony will or will not go. Most ponies know what ground will bear them and either refuse, or are very reluctant, to go on ground which is too soft. As a general rule, if a stalking stick can be pushed down into the ground a depth of a foot or two, then the ground is too soft: if, on pushing down the stick, a firm basis is found on several adjacent prods, then the ground is probably all right. Ground with a good grass cover, and certainly ground with heather on it, and wettish ground through which the stones are showing, are all suitable, but peat hags and bogs must be avoided. The weight on each foot of a pony, especially when loaded, is very much more than the weight on a human foot, so the fact that a human can walk over the ground is no real test, except to say that, if the ground shudders as if it were floating, then it probably is, and it will be quite unsafe for the pony.

In addition to a pony, there are now various forms of mechanical hill transport. These fall into two classes, first, the wheeled transport and second, those with tracks.

It is not the intention of this book to recommend one sort more than the other, but some observations may be helpful though, in selecting the best transport for any particular forest, the reader should consult the appropriate dealers (the difficulty being that most of the dealers supply one particular sort and not the others). However, they are mostly to be seen at the game fair and like gatherings.

Probably the best known of the wheeled transport is the 'Argo-cat'; this has been aptly described as an enlarged plastic bath on wheels. It is in fact a rectangular plastic body on six or eight low-pressure wheels, all of which drive: the steering is achieved by braking on the wheels on one side or the other. After original teething troubles, this transport has now been developed into a very reliable hill transport, which will go practically anywhere on the hill except over big rocks. These should be avoided, because they damage the body (in spite of aluminium shields) and also the tyres, which are balloon, very low-pressure tyres, running at about 3lb/sq inch (0.21kg/cm²). The four-stroke engine produces a low-tone noise which, for some reason, does not seem to attract the attention of the deer nearly so much as the higher revving engines or two-stroke engines formerly used. It looks very small, but will carry two adults and three stags as a maximum: to carry more is over-taxing it. When it does get stuck, which is seldom, it is light enough to be manhandled by two people out of the difficulty. It is an excellent hill transport but, because of its lightness, and although the construction is sound, I doubt if it will last many seasons of hard wear. It has the added advantage that it can be fitted with tracks over the wheels for work in snow: it is very little use in snow which is at all deep without tracks.

In this category too is the 'Gnat', which is a three-wheeled vehicle on balloon low-pressure tyres, the main defect of which is a tendency to tip over when traversing steep sides of the hill. Another good wheeled vehicle is the 'Limpet', which is really a small platform lorry with double agricultural wheels at the back. I have no experience of this machine, but have had good reports.

Of the tracked vehicles, the best known is the 'Snowtrac'. This has more than ample carrying capacity but it is a very heavy, as well as expensive, vehicle. It, too, goes practically anywhere, having ample power and a very good grip on its tracks but its great disadvantage, beyond its price, is its weight for, if it is stuck, or breaks down, there is nothing that will move it except another Snowtrac.

There are also other tracked vehicles on the market smaller than the Snowtrac, though such of these as I have tried, while behaving admirably on a show ground, have not been up to conditions on the hill over long periods. One depended on nylon teeth, in which driving sprockets engaged, but these teeth broke at an alarming rate though, it is true, this was under snow and freezing conditions, when nylon and various other plastics become harder and more brittle because of the cold. No doubt, that will be remedied or may, indeed, already have been remedied, but it goes to show that, before expending large or quite large sums on hill transport, it should be tested under all conditions actually on the hill.

Finally, where not a great many deer are to be got in, a simple 'barrow' or, as it is sometimes called, 'deer bicycle', can readily be made of a structure rather like a stretcher on top with a single bicycle wheel, or better still moped wheel, underneath and in the middle. Two people can fairly readily transport a stag on this, each holding the shafts at either side, one at the front and one at the back, just as a stretcher is carried: the wheel takes the weight of the stag. This is far better than dragging but it does, of course, have the disadvantage that it has got to be taken up the hill with the stalking party. A motorised version of this can also be made, using an ordinary lawn-mower engine geared down to walking speed. If so geared down, 2 or 2½ hp (1·5kW or 1·9kW) is quite sufficient.

8

THE SHOT

Having obtained and tested the equipment, the next thing is to put it into practice. The actual shot is normally taken from the prone position or, especially for downhill shots, the sitting position with the elbows resting on the knees: both these methods should be practised and mastered. A standing shot from the shoulder is very seldom used, except to finish off a deer which may, unfortunately, have been wounded.

The object is to get a clean kill and, therefore, nothing that assists in this should be rejected. If you shoot better using a sling round the arm then it should be used and, similarly, the assistance of a bag or other small object to rest the forearm on makes for addition- al stability. The elbows and hand holding the rifle, or the rifle itself, should never be rested on bare rock. The reason for this is that the sighting of the rifle allows for a certain amount of 'give' on the recoil and, to get this, the elbows, hand or rifle must be rested on something soft and not entirely unyielding.

It is of the utmost importance with a telescopic sight to make sure that the line of fire in front of the muzzle of the rifle is entirely clear, not only of any rock, but of all grass, heather or other herbage. This is by no means as easy as it sounds, because the telescopic sight is above the line of fire and, when one is peeping over the brow of a hillock cautiously, it is very easy to have the line of fire immediately in front of the muzzle just too low. Rock, of course, will obviously deflect the bullet and may, indeed, be even dangerous, but many people do not realise that even a rush or bit of grass can and does give a deflection to the bullet as it leaves the muzzle, because of its very high velocity. It is, therefore, absolutely essential to be certain that the pathway of the bullet is entirely clear, which may be a different thing from failing to see any obstruction through the telescopic sight.

Although the stalker will know where to shoot, and will endeavour to give the novice a broadside shot, sooner or later shots at different angles will have to be taken and, therefore, it is important to have a reasonable knowledge of the anatomy of deer. One of the best ways of amusing oneself in the evening before stalking is to look at pictures of deer and decide where various deer could be shot. This will avoid a whispered conversation with the stalker at the last minute, which is not to be desired from the stalking point of view, in any case, and may lead to confusion if the gentleman is unused to a Scottish accent.

Considering the number of deer which are shot each year, it is surprising how much argument goes on about what is the best shot; and this has been further complicated by the recent increase in the price of venison, and the desire not to spoil any meat. One now hears a head shot advocated sometimes, but that is not a shot which should be taken on the hill, except at very close range or by a very experienced shot. The reason for this is simple, when the anatomy of the head is considered. The brain is situated between the eyes and the ears, and slightly further back than the ears, but not going very far down the head if looked at sideways. A very slight deviation downwards will, therefore, go through the lower jaw of the unfortunate beast, who will then go off very strongly and for a very long way, and be most difficult to catch up with again. It will, of course, ultimately die, though I have twice found beasts with .22 bullets embedded in their lower jaw, alive and apparently well. These were undoubtedly poachers' .22 bullets, and it is horrifying to think of the suffering which must have been inflicted on these unfortunate deer before they ultimately recovered and were able to eat again properly.

Hinds at ease

The right shot to kill a deer is a heart shot. Fortunately, the heart is easy to locate (although not visible) in a beast standing broadside on with its near front leg vertical. Simply follow up the back of the front leg, and half way up the body, above the point of the shoulder, is the top of the heart, and that is the right place to shoot for. Surrounding the heart are the lungs, and above that the backbone. A shot, therefore, at the top of the heart, if it goes slightly high, will either go through the lungs or hit the backbone; if it goes slightly low, it will go right through the heart and/or lungs; and if it goes slightly forward or back it will also be through the lungs. In addition to that, the spreading out of the bullet on impact will probably cause it to go through all these organs. They are all extremely sensitive and, therefore, the shock effect is very great, and all are fatal shots. That shot, therefore, allows the greatest margin of error, while still being fatal immediately.

A neck shot may also be taken but, here, much more accuracy is required because, to be fatal, it must go through the backbone and shatter the spinal column. There is not sufficient resistance to cause the bullet to expand properly through the fleshy part of the neck, especially if it goes through the windpipe, which takes up most of the lower half of the neck below the spinal column. That will produce a nasty wound but it will be extremely difficult to catch up with the deer again. At close range, a shot just where the neck joins the head, so that it severs the spinal column there, is undoubtedly fatal and is a good shot but the target is very small, because that is the narrowest part of the neck. However, if it is close, then that is a fatal shot and spoils no meat. It is far better than a shot at the head itself.

Those who go stalking must be able to work out from the anatomy of the deer where to aim on the surface of the animal to reach the heart. When shooting at an angle, it is necessary to bear in mind the effect of the heavy bones, particularly the shoulder bone. In the olden days, when bullets were not so fast, the shoulder bone frequently stopped a bullet. Nowadays, this is rare but by no means unheard of, particularly if the bullet hits just where the T part of the shoulder sticks out. If the shoulder does stop the bullet, then the shock is very considerable, but by no means fatal. The deer will fall, probably, but will get up again and go on. Secondly, bullets can ricochet off a shoulder bone or rib-cage and, in that case, they will not penetrate in the line expected but will probably go down inside the rib-cage and finish up in the stomach. There is not much one can do about either of these, except to bear them in mind and get another shot in quickly should either occur; but one of my reasons for disliking the lighter, higher velocity bullet, such as the .243 or .240, is that both these things are more likely to occur with such a bullet, which gets its energy content more from the velocity and less from the weight of the bullet.

The professional stalker, watching through his binoculars, should see the strike of the bullet on the deer, usually by a sort of puff of hair: he should also know from its reaction whether it has been hit, and where. However, this is such a vitally important matter that the person shooting should also know, and be ready to act accordingly although, after any shot, the rifle should always be reloaded immediately. In general, the reactions of deer to the shot are as follows:

If shot through the heart, the deer gives the impression of jerking itself together and makes a large jump into the air, all four feet leaving the ground. It then rushes off in the direction in which it happens to be facing, at full gallop, for perhaps 50yd (45m) and falls down indisputably dead. This all happens much more quickly than it takes to say it and I have no doubt at all that, under these circumstances, although it does cover the 50 yards or so, the deer feels absolutely nothing.

Getting into position for the shot

If shot through the backbone, so that the spinal column is affected, the deer falls immediately, and lies still.

If shot through the lungs (without either the heart or the back-bone being touched) or if shot through the liver, which lies just behind the lungs, the deer will apparently pull itself together in much the same way as for a heart shot. It will probably not jump, though it may, and it will rush off at full gallop: it will then stop and stand swaying. If it is seen to be definitely swaying, there is no need to take any further action, and it will fall down dead. The gallop may be slightly longer than in the case of a shot actually through the heart but, again, I am convinced that the deer has no idea what has happened, nor do I think that it has time to feel pain because, in this case, it dies partly from shock and partly from the loss of blood to the brain, due to heavy internal bleeding from lungs or liver. It will be noticed that I have now brought in the liver, which I did not mention earlier: a liver shot is normally fatal, but it is not one to be encouraged. The bullet must expand a good deal before going into the liver to create a substantial wound and get enough internal bleeding to affect the blood supply to the brain.

In addition to the visual indications, the bullet may usually be heard hitting the deer; if it hits the rib-cage a sharp 'plop' can be heard. If it, unfortunately, hits too far back in the stomach region, then there is what one can only describe as a much more deep cross between a plop and a thud. A shot in the neck makes practically no sound. But a warning should be added that a bullet, if it misses a deer, can make a plop sound on entering soft, wet ground so that the sound, although very valuable, and particularly encouraging to spectators out of sight of the actual shot, should only be used as confirmation of visual observation.

Every effort should be made to avoid wounding deer but, even more important, every effort must be made to kill any deer which should, unfortunately, be wounded and, if one knows where it is wounded and what to look for, the suffering of the poor beast can be made either negligible or very short.

Rule number one is, undoubtedly, that if a beast falls immediately, as if shot through the spine (including the neck), always reload quickly and stay ready to shoot again for much longer than you think necessary. The reason for this is that, if the bullet has just grazed the spine and not affected the actual spinal column, the shock will still be very great but will be short-lived: the beast will fall, but will recover again and go off as if it had never been shot. The fall is so instantantaneous, and the animal looks so indubitably dead, that the tendency is to get up and go towards it, or otherwise take one's attention off it; but, under these circumstances, they can lie for a matter of seconds up to even five or ten minutes and still be capable of getting up quite suddenly and going off very rapidly. This is, perhaps, especially so if the beast is lying on its back and waving its legs in the air, which is normally an indication that it is dead and merely subject to some reaction from the automatic part of the brain.

Such accidents as happen occasionally out stalking usually occur when the stalker walks up to a deer lying like this, which has fallen immediately and, as he gets very close, the deer comes to. Under these circumstances, it will attack, and may inflict a serious, if not fatal, wound with its horns, although this is rare. Incidentally, it is best to touch the deer's eye with a stick first of all to see if there is any reaction. It is also as well to know that a deer cannot get up if its back leg is held off the ground because it always gets up back legs first. If it does, therefore, come to, and there are two people, one should immediately take hold of the back leg and keep it off the ground at all costs.

If a deer should be shot in the shoulder, the bullet will normally penetrate either to the spine or the heart or lungs, or possibly all of them, because it will break up a good deal but, if it does lodge in the shoulder, as is occasionally possible (as mentioned above), the shock is very considerable, and the deer normally falls as if shot in the spine. Under these circumstances, the time that it will lie still as if dead varies very much more, and can be quite considerable. A wound can often be seen on the shoulder, probably bleeding, and there is a great tendency to think the deer is dead; but I can recall at least one occasion when this happened and the deer lay for quite ten minutes and then got up, stood looking dazed while the shock wore off, and then went off rather unsteadily, but recovering quickly as it went. On this occasion, I was merely a spectator, and the stalker and rifle were crossing the corrie across which the shot had been taken and were out of sight of the deer when all this happened. They were very surprised when I ran on and caught them up just as they got to where they thought the deer was. I am glad to add that we did get it after a very long chase but, had we waited a little longer at the original firing point, there would have been no difficulty in shooting the deer again when it first got up.

The most deceiving wound is probably one where a heart shot is taken, but it is too low and goes through the bottom of the rib-cage or foreleg. In this case, the deer will give a jump very much like the jump characteristic of a heart shot, but without the quick sort of pulling together of its whole body, which is also characteristic of the heart shot. After the jump, it goes off, and one may look for it to fall as for a heart shot, but it does not do so, because that shot is by no means fatal, and the deer will go a long way. If, therefore, one thinks one has shot through the heart, but the deer does not behave characteristically in falling, another shot should be taken as quickly as possible: nothing is wasted except a little extra meat, and that is of no consequence compared to a wounded beast. In fact, the strike of the shot will probably not have been heard either, because the plop is either absent or not nearly so loud.

If the shot is too far back and through the stomach, the deer will generally stand or start to move off very slowly, and a very definite hollow plop of the bullet hitting the deer will almost certainly have been heard. In these circumstances, another shot should be taken again, as soon as possible, but do not get into a panic and shoot too quickly, so that it is wounded again. A deer shot through the stomach can travel a very long way before it dies, but it will not do so unless it has been frightened more than one shot will have frightened it. It will not know what the first shot is; it will be feeling very sick and, therefore, the tendency will be to lie down or to move off slowly. The stalker should, therefore, be quite sure of the second shot rather than get into a panic and fire too many shots to no effect, except to frighten the deer to the extent that it will exert all its remaining energy to escape.

If, therefore, a deer is moving off slowly after a shot and another shot is not possible, for instance, if it is tail-on going over the top of a brow of a hill, or if it has gone on and you can see it lying down with its head up (which is a point you must always look for), then it should be re-stalked carefully and a careful shot taken to kill it. Do not, in any case, panic yourself, or panic the deer by giving it an enormous fright so that it really realises what is going on. This advice applies to all wounded deer: if they can be seen, they should be stalked with the greatest care. Equally, if going over a ridge to see whether a deer has fallen or gone on, great care should be taken not to appear on the skyline until it has been ascertained that the animal is actually dead.

It cannot be over-emphasised that wounded deer must be followed and must be followed carefully, though as rapidly as possible and, in this respect, a dog is of the greatest help because the deer which are lost wounded, though there are very few, are lost because they have gone over a ridge or something like that after the shot, and it is not known which way they have gone after going out of sight. Any trained dog, particularly a labrador, will very rapidly know which deer to follow, especially if there is the odd drop of blood, and then it must be followed with the greatest care, spying very carefully, because there will be no difficulty getting it if it has lain down, as they usually do, and it is seen lying down before it sees, hears or smells you.

The recovery of wounded deer is so important, although every attempts should be made not to wound any, that the 'rules' should perhaps be re-stated in brief:

(a)   If the deer gallops a short way and then falls, either straight away or after a moment or two of swaying, it is virtually certain to be dead.

(b)   If it falls straight away, it should be watched carefully and shot immediately if it attempts to rise, or immediately it has risen.

(c)   If it stands, or goes off slowly looking sickly, take care and plenty of time for another careful shot.

(d)   If it jumps, runs, but does not fall, it is almost certainly grazed in the bottom of the chest, and should be shot as quickly as possible, because it will go a long way.

(e)   A wounded deer should never be frightened more. If, therefore, it can be seen (for instance, if there is an open corrie or hillside) do not move, but watch it carefully until it lies down, and then re-stalk carefully. If it does go out of sight, for instance, over a ridge, go up on to the ridge, or some other vantage point, as quickly as possible, but taking particular care as you go over the ridge, for it may be lying just the other side. Then watch until it lies down and re-stalk, or take a careful shot.

(f)   Never rush after deer in the open, unless you are certain of getting a shot: it will be almost certain to see you, and will redouble its efforts to get away. It will be capable of very much more effort than you think.

(g)   If there are two of you, it is a good thing for one to sit and watch the deer while the other goes round out of sight to re-stalk it, or re-stalk where it is thought to be coming; but the two must arrange some means of keeping in contact, the watcher indicating to the other what to do when he cannot see the deer.

(h)   A wounded deer lies down in a peat hag or a steep burn which it finds difficult to cross: the greatest care must therefore be taken in such places, so that you see the deer first, before it sees you.

(i)   A deer which lies down (as opposed to falling) is very likely to be capable of getting up again, and must be treated with the greatest care, as above, especially if it has its head up.

No mention has been made of a shot in the haunch. That should never occur, and it is for this reason that a shot should not be taken in the breast of a deer facing the rifle directly because, although it will go through the heart and lungs, so killing the deer, it will finish up in the haunches as well. That shot is, of course, permissible if the deer has already been wounded, emphasis then being on getting it quickly.

Care must always be taken to see that the shot intended for one

Old or middle-aged stags: one good, one bad. Neither of these stags can safely be shot for fear of wounding the other, unless the shooter is absolutely sure of a shot in the neck of the left-hand one

beast does not wound another, either after it has gone through the first (and it should be remembered that it may be deflected on passage through the first beast) or by a slight error in direction or elevation.

Finally, everybody knows, or should know, that the trigger of a rifle must be squeezed and not pulled, but a hint for those who shoot with a shotgun as well (where the action is much quicker, and who find that sooner or later, through this, they pull a rifle trigger instead of squeezing it), it is virtually impossible to pull a rifle trigger if only the tip of the top joint of the trigger finger is used in actual contact with the trigger.

9
PRINCIPLES AND PRACTICE
OF STALKING

No people take greater trouble to see that unnecessary suffering is never inflicted upon their quarry than do stalkers and therefore, before going on the hill, it is absolutely essential for all stalkers to make quite sure not only that they are competent shots, but that the rifle and sighting are correct. This question is dealt with in another chapter but it is so vitally important that no apologies are made for repetition here.

Furthermore, it is also essential for the stalker to know the various positions from which he may be asked to shoot, and to be certain that he can get into these positions comfortably, and handle the rifle properly from these attitudes. The main positions of firing will be either the prone position or the sitting position, resting the elbows on the knees. It is not likely that it will be necessary to take a shot from the standing position without a rest except, possibly, to finish off a beast, but the stalker should be certain that he can take up all these positions and shoot accurately from them, or at least that he can shoot from the prone position and the sitting position. Those who have only shot at a target or on a range may not have realised the necessity for the sitting position, especially where firing steeply downhill.

Hinds getting restless

A person may, as a result of injury, an operation or age, have limitation of movement somewhere, particularly the movement of getting the head well back. In this case, he will find difficulty shooting uphill from a prone position, unless he can find a suitable hillock to raise the front of his body so that the line of fire is a straight line from the line of his body, and not at an angle above this line. There is nothing wrong in this, and no reason why somebody suffering any such minor limitation should not stalk, but it is absolutely vital that he should know his limitations, and tell the professional stalker of them, so that a suitable firing position may be found. The professional stalker seldom believes this, but it is absolutely essential to impress it upon him, otherwise the shot will be taken from an uncomfortable angle, which is usually disastrous.

A much more common thing is for the stalker to shoot from his left shoulder (as I do) instead of his right. Here again, it is essential to inform the professional stalker, because the other side of the small knoll to the one preferred by a right-shouldered shot is much more comfortable, and gives a much more steady shot. Again, I add a particular plea to professional stalkers to bear this in mind as they take their gentleman up. It is not nonsense: a left-hand shot lies at a different angle from a right-hand shot.

All this may sound unnecessary fuss to some but, in fact, it is not, because it takes us back to the first sentence, that it is essential to make sure of a clean kill when out stalking.

There is a very small minority of people who glory in taking a long shot, because they think they are very good shots or that there is some great merit in getting a stag with a wonderful long shot, but this is not the object of stalking and the person who adopts this attitude would do better to go to Bisley. The object of stalking is just that, to stalk within a reasonable distance of the deer; and that is part of the skill and pleasure of it, as well as the skill and pleasure of selecting the right beast to stalk, as described elsewhere, and the pleasure of being out on the hill. One should, therefore, get as close to the deer as reasonably practicable.

That means, in general, a range of between 75 and 150yd (70–140m), or possibly 200yd (180m). In many circumstances, it is possible to get closer than 75yd (70m) but, at shorter ranges than this, the deer, which have very acute hearing, will almost certainly hear something and, if they have not moved off, at any rate be on the alert. They also have acute sight, especially for movement and, at short range, will see the slightest movement, so that it is almost impossible to put the rifle up. The ideal range is 100 to 150yd (90–140m), when, if one is careful and moves slowly, not showing too much of the body or rifle, one should be able to get plenty of time to take a comfortable shot and to select the right beast and so on, without haste.

There are circumstances of terrain where it is impossible to get within 200yd (180m) of deer, especially where they are on the far side of a wide, open valley, or on the far side of a concave hill face with no suitable burns or hillocks to give cover. In these circumstances, it is better not to attempt the stalk, but to go for another lot of deer. There may be exceptional circumstances where a longer shot is necessary. For instance, if a large hummel is rutting with a good lot of hinds, one might take that up to 300yd (270m), provided the stalker was absolutely sure of his shot, but it should certainly not be done with a good stag. Equally, of course, a longer shot may be taken if one is unfortunate enough to wound a beast

Modern rifles are perfectly accurate to many hundreds of yards but the sight will be set to 100 or 200yd (90–180m) and, after that, distance allowance will have to be made for the drop of the bullet and, possibly, also for windage, if there is at all a strong wind. In addition to that, the rifle barrel may be beginning to be slightly worn and, though it will fire accurately at normal ranges, it may not be as accurate as thought for longer ranges. All these things add complications which, for the good name of stalking, and the fact that clean kills are the rule, should not be allowed to enter into the matter.

Having, therefore, taken all precautions to get a clean kill, we can set out on our stalk to try and get into a position to shoot a suitable stag. How to do this depends largely on the forest but, in general, it will be desirable to go up the hill sufficiently far to get a good spy, that is to say, to get on to some vantage point where one can see much of the forest at a range of half a mile (0.80km) to 3 or 4 miles (5–6km). Some forests lend themselves to this more than others, and there will always be places like the flat tops of hills which cannot be adequately spied at long range. Nevertheless, it is very important, and adds greatly to the pleasure, to be able to get a good spy of the ground ahead, because then one can see all the lots of deer that are available for stalking, look at the stags' heads, discuss means of getting in and so on. Old-fashioned stalkers tended to think that their duties began and ended in merely taking their gentleman up to a suitable position, handing him the rifle, usually cocked, pointing out the stag and merely expecting him to pull the trigger. This, fortunately, is now nearly obsolete and, provided that the gentleman in question has taken the trouble to find out what he is likely to do by way of stalking, the professional stalker, if encouraged, is usually fully prepared to discuss the day's stalking prospects and other matters. That, of course, largely depends on the approach to him, because many Highlanders are reticent, but it does add enormously to the pleasure of the day and general interest, for both parties to discuss it.

Deer use all three senses to ascertain danger. Their sense of smell is extraordinarily acute, particularly when smelling scent carried by the wind: in a force 3 or 4 wind, they can smell human beings upwind of them for up to two miles at least and, once they have smelt humans, they will go off without hesitation, and go a considerable way. It is, therefore, quite disastrous to allow them to get the wind.

Their hearing is also good but by no means exceptional, though it is better than good human hearing, and they are particularly good at the higher ranges. Thus, they hear female, high-pitched voices better than a low-pitched male whisper. When deer are being photographed under still conditions or very light wind, they will hear a camera shutter at 50 to 75yd (45–70m), but will not go off. They will merely look up and look in the direction of the noise because they have been made suspicious. Their reaction then depends on what follows next: if, for instance, they see as well as hear the person making the noise, they will probably then go off.

They can see about as well as a human being with good sight. That is to say, if you have good sight, and you can see the deer, they can probably see you, too, so it is not safe to move in the open where you can see the deer. There is, however, this qualification, that they are much more perceptive, and afraid, of movement than of something which remains still, even at comparatively close range: Provided you remain absolutely still, they will often merely stare at you and, ultimately, settle down again. If, therefore, during a stalk, one or more deer put their heads up and look in your direction, it is absolutely essential to remain entirely motionless until you have, as the old stalker put it, 'stared the deer out'. In the course of a stalk, therefore, if the stalker stops within the sight of the deer, you must stop too, *when* he stops, not where he stops. Many a stalk has been ruined by the gentleman catching up with the professional stalker and stopping alongside him, or even moving about to find a less wet place to sit in (for this sort of moment always seems to occur when one is in the middle of a bog!).

Because deer have such an acute sense of smell, you will have started a stalk from the leeward side of the forest, if possible, and will be spying upwind; or, if it is not possible to get round that side to start, you will have gone up crosswind, so will be either spying upwind or across the wind. It is at this stage that the professional stalker, who knows the ground, will find the deer much quicker than the stalker who does not, but even the latter can do a good deal about knowing where to look first of all, which is half the battle of finding the deer quickly or, indeed, at all. Many people are amazed how quickly the stalker finds the deer, but that is mainly a question of knowing where to look. Fortunately, deer like to be where they have a good view downwind (which is the way we are), because they can sense danger approaching from the other direction by means of

An old hind (foreground) starting to move off while the middle-aged hind and stag remain suspicious and curious

their sense of smell, but must rely on their sight for danger approaching on their downwind side.

Each herd of deer will have one or two look-out deer; the latter will be high up the face, if the deer are on a face, or on top of some little knoll, where they have a good view downwind. This is fortunate, because they are much easier to see in this position than if they are lying down in the heather or among the rocks. The deer, on the whole, favour shelter rather than being out in the wind, and the places to look first are the sheltered corries and sheltered sides of the knolls, looking especially on the top of the little knolls which themselves provide shelter.

What one looks for is a combination of shape and colour: there are always plenty of bits of grass, dying moss, brown rock, etc, of the right colour, so the colour alone is no clue, and only experience can get one used to the shape of deer in their various attitudes. After a bit, it becomes almost second nature but, at first, one must, having found something of the right size and colour, try and make out which is the head, rump, legs and so on, and which way it is facing. This applies especially if it is thought to be lying down, for deer seldom stand long in one place, and movement relative to some other feature in the landscape can almost always be detected within a short time if the deer is thought to be standing. Single deer lying down are undoubtedly the most difficult to detect, but their heads can nearly always be made out with careful looking, and a single deer will seldom lie long in the daytime with its head down: they are much too wary to be caught like that!

Having scanned quickly the likely places, one then scans the whole of the hillside visible, and it is a matter of personal choice whether one traverses it with the glasses horizontally or in vertical strips. Some people do one, some the other, but it is most important to do it on a methodical pattern to be sure that one has looked carefully at the whole of the hillside, and not too rapidly. It is important to get a picture of the whole of the deer population of the hillside when spying, and not just one herd of deer which may stand out prominently. Many stalkers will prefer to do this themselves first, before pointing out any deer to their companion. This is not a matter of being obstinate or mysterious, it is simply to get a full picture, which is most difficult against a background of interruptions: so do not be impatient, as proper spying is of the greatest importance.

Even with 8X binoculars, good-bodied stags will stand out easily in comparison to hinds at two or three miles (3 to 5km) but, at this range, it will be necessary to look again with the telescope to see the exact head which each stag carries. Having done all that, one can then decide which to stalk, and which it is impossible to stalk, either because there are other deer in the way, or because the particular herd one wishes to stalk is on the far side of very open or concave ground, the latter being the most difficult.

It should, of course, be remembered that wind eddies and, therefore, although one may be directly downwind of the deer, it is not necessary for the wind to be blowing that way where the deer are lying. If there are wisps of mist about, then the direction of the wind can be seen from the travel of the mist. However, since that is the only use of the mist, it is to be hoped that there will be none. Another indication of the direction of the wind where the deer are lying is from the position of the deer themselves: those lying down prefer to lie with their backs to the wind. Their fur slopes backwards, so they do not like the wind blowing actually up their backs but, when they are lying down, the tops of their backs tend, on the whole, to be towards the direction of the wind. Their position is dictated, to some extent, by the slope and shape of the ground where they are, so that there will be deer lying in several different positions. But, by taking the right ones, and by taking a sort of average from experience, one can often get a very good idea of the direction of any wind there is where the deer are lying. This is a matter which one can only learn from experience but, by looking at the deer and trying to make up one's mind when one is spying, and then checking up after one has reached where the deer were and had the shot, one can gain experience quickly for a future occasion and, by practising this, again, additional pleasure can be had.

We now come to the actual stalk: in other words, having decided which of the herds of deer one is going to approach, one plans a route to keep out of sight of the deer. Previous experience of which of the burns afford sufficient cover and which of the hillocks will keep one out of sight of where the deer are is of great assistance: but, if one has to stalk on strange ground, it is still possible, by considering it carefully through the binoculars, and being prepared to go so far and then, if necessary, come back and try another way. Ideally, if one has to move in sight of the deer, such movement should be done when one is as far as possible away from them, rather than when one is near them. That is to say, that, between alternative routes, the best one to choose is that where any movement in sight of the deer is at extreme range, rather than one where the movement in sight of the deer will be closer to them.

It also has to borne in mind that one not only has to stalk the deer to be shot, but also any other deer which may be in the way, by keeping out of sight and scent of these deer as well. For, if one lot of deer starts moving, it will move all other deer within sight. That applies to both deer one has been able to see, or any deer which may be on land which one could not spy in the intervening area. Therefore, when walking over ground which could not be seen from the original spy-point, it is of the utmost importance to go very slowly and carefully, and to avoid skylines as far as possible, where one is most visible. To those used to going on the hills to see the view, the natural thing to do is to go over the top of any little hillock but this must not be done when stalking. Always go round the side of the hillocks so as to avoid coming over the skyline, and go very slowly at those points where new ground comes into sight.

It is always preferable to take the longer way round to keep out of sight than to risk crossing ground in view of the deer, even if quite a long way off. It is much quicker to walk half-a-mile (0.80km) round than to have to crawl even 200yd (180m). It may be possible to walk right up to within shot of the deer, and only have to crawl the last few yards over an intervening hillock but, if so, one is very lucky, though the novice will think that stalking is all too easy if the first stalk turns out like this. There is nearly always a point in stalking where it is essential to crawl, and to crawl slowly, for the quicker the movement, the more the deer see it. Also, the flatter one is to the ground, the less there is for them to see, and the less do they recognise what they do see (if they see anything) as a human being, which they normally think of as being erect. This is not to say that they do not recognise a crawling figure as being human quite soon enough: they certainly do, but not as readily, by any means, as an erect figure.

When one is forced to crawl within sight of the deer, the stalker should go in front (as he normally does), the gentleman following as close as possible behind. The stalker will keep his eye on the deer and watch to see if any of them have seen something: they can put their heads up remarkably fast, so that it is essential to be prepared to stop immediately. A deer that has seen something suspicious looks directly at it, facing it, but if there is no further movement, it will generally turn away and go on with its grazing. This, of course, is all right if the deer are grazing. If, however, some are lying down, they may be facing the direction of the stalk in any case, which will make it very much more difficult to watch them closely and detect when they have seen something suspicious. Nevertheless, even in these circumstances, their facial expression changes to one of much more interest. Stalking in sight of the deer is a very thrilling and interesting experience, but it should only be undertaken as a last resort, or over short distances, because the chances of success are reduced substantially once they have had their suspicions aroused, and they will look back in the direction they thought they saw something again and again.

Whether one has to crawl on all fours or on one's stomach depends on the nature of the terrain, and some forests are much more open, some more broken, with lots of little hillocks and deep burns to go up. One takes advantage of any burn there is, having spied it out beforehand to see that it runs sufficiently deep and as far as necessary. Burns have an irritating habit of running deep for just a short way and then running out over a flat piece of ground.

As one is stalking, so far as possible out of sight of the deer, it is most important when one spies them originally and sets out on the stalk, to pick out for oneself some landmark which will be conspicuous during the stalk, such as a prominent rock or something of that nature, just above the deer. One hillock has a most irritating habit of looking just like another hillock when one gets close to it, or from a different angle, so that it is vitally important to have a distinguishing landmark which will guide one to the place where one wishes to be, without continually having to come into sight of the deer to make certain where they are. Of course, when merely following a stalker, it will appear easy, because he will know the ground by heart and be able to move up to his chosen firing point without difficulty. However, one must remember that this takes a good deal of doing and, if one is stalking alone, then the selection of good landmarks for each stage of the stalk, chosen with care from the original spy point, or some other vantage point early on in the stalk, is of enormous advantage. It is a help to practise taking marks when one plans a stalk with the stalker, then, when on one's own, one is more used to selecting them, not to mention finding them, (because rocks have a nasty habit of looking quite different from different angles!). One mark, for instance, should be where one is to leave the burn, possibly a white stone in the burn, and a couple more marks to guide one to the firing point, out of sight of the deer. Failure to do this has led to many amateur stalkers finding themselves in front of the deer, with disastrous results, because the deer are then, of course, upwind.

That is the practice of the straightforward stalk, where one has been able to get a good spy to begin with. As has been indicated, there are many forests, and many places in forests, where there is much dead ground which cannot be spied adequately in advance. Here, great care is necessary, and the tips already mentioned about never coming over the skyline if possible, but coming round the hill instead, should be followed as far as practicable. It is also essential to spy continually with binoculars and notice when fresh ground is opening up into view.

The tendency is to spy from one place, and then get a good deal higher and have another spy, but that is nearly always disastrous, because the deer will have been just out of sight on the first spy, and so will be well in view on the second one! Such is the perversity of things on the hill that, in these circumstances, one may have got to the second spy point without being seen by the deer, but they will certainly see the slightest movement as a cautious retreat is attempted! By the nature of the ground, they will be reasonably close, and will then go off, probably taking other deer with them.

In this type of situation, the necessities are either extremely good and quick eyesight, or very frequent spies with binoculars. Due to the nature of the terrain, the stalk is not usually so difficult, except in the case of hills with even, but slightly rounded, tops, where the last few yards are extremely difficult, in order to get oneself high enough up to shoot without shooting the ground in front (see Chapter 7 on rifles and stalking equipment, where the problems of the actual shot are dealt with).

No mention so far has been made of the weather. The light, of course, affects stalking very much: on the whole, the better the light, the more the stalker is favoured because, with the aid of binoculars and telescope, he can see the deer further off, and select his beast more easily. However, at closer range, it makes little difference because both the stalker and the deer are about equally affected. The effect of any sunlight should be borne in mind: both deer and stalkers can see best with the sun behind them, and worst straight into the sun. This is a feature which may be taken into account and used successfully by the stalker but there are other disadvantages of sunlight which must always be remembered on the high hill. First, where one's shadow is falling. It is no use stalking deer with great care and keeping out of sight if one's shadow falls half way down the hill in full sight of them, and walks along as one progresses: the deer will know all about shadows which they can see. Secondly, sunlight reflects and flashes from rifle barrels, stocks (if polished), telescopes and binocular lenses etc, and nothing is seen more easily.

Provided one is properly clad, rain is an enemy only as far as it affects telescopes, binoculars and telescopic sights. However, it does affect all optical instruments to a greater or lesser degree. Nothing can be done about it, except to try and spy in fine intervals, and it is always as well, if spying has to be done in the rain, for one member of the party to spy, keeping the other's glasses dry for future use. Another useful tip is to take a good supply of paper handkerchiefs for drying glasses in these circumstances.

The greatest enemy of stalking is mist or fog or, as some people prefer to call it, low cloud. It is, in fact, all the same. On a short stalking visit, there is a great temptation to go on stalking through the mist, hoping for the best. However, that is a great mistake, since things are then loaded much in favour of the deer with their excellent sense of smell and hearing. If one pushes on, a time is almost certain to arrive when deer will be downwind one side or the other, get the wind and go off. They will be very apt to make upwind, where they can smell other deer, or where other deer will hear them going off at a gallop. They will move further, and are always more restless in the mist, because of their lack of vision and it is all too easy to clear the forest or the beat of deer, and so spoil the following day.

Many people say that deer can see better through the mist than human beings. This is probably not, in fact, true if one takes a human with good sight but what is very visible through the mist is movement of a figure on the skyline. Because the stalking party is moving, and the deer are probably not, it is the stalking party which gets seen and not the reverse. The best thing to do is to decide whether the mist is likely to clear (it is hoped that the chapter on this subject may help) and, if one thinks it will clear, then sit down and wait. If it is not going to clear, the sensible thing is either to give up and go home or to get below the mist and do such stalking as may be available at that level.

There are exceptions to this, and it may be necessary to stalk in the mist where the numbers are down, towards the end of the season. In this case, the stags will be roaring, and that puts the situation very much more in favour of the stalker, because he can hear where the deer, or at least some of the deer, are.

Another way in which the tables can be turned on the deer in rain or mist, and to a lesser, but by no means negligible, extent when stalking fairly blind ground, is by taking a dog. The average intelligent labrador will very quickly learn what the quarry is, and will snuff the air in a characteristic way when deer are ahead. They can smell deer an incredible way off upwind, and soon learn the principles of stalking if taken out a few times. The owner who has a close rapport with his dog soon gets to appreciate the signals which his dog is making, and it adds greatly to the pleasure and success of stalking, as well as avoiding the awful parting on leaving the dog behind. The dog must, of course, be steady, and must on no account whine when left sitting. That is a thing some dogs suffer from: it is very difficult to stop and sure to spoil the stalk, because the deer hear a high-pitched whine a long way off.

I remember, particularly, two stalks in the mist. The first was, perhaps, not a stalk at all, but it was a memorable day. I had been deputed by a friend, who very kindly let me do, virtually, second stalker on his forest when I was there, to take another friend out, with our respective wives as followers. We were allotted a long glen, with some side glens off it, as our beat for the day. We left the car at the bottom, where the track ended, and set off up the glen with low cloud on the top of the hills. This gradually lowered as a warm front came in. We could spy nothing in the glen below the cloud, so we decided to go up a side glen which, as I knew, became a steep-sided burn towards the top, where we sat down to wait for a clearance and have our lunch. We chose this place because it was sheltered, most of the wind blowing right over the top at right angles to the valley, such wind as there was in the bottom eddying up the valley, and we had done most of our climb for the time when the mist cleared.

While we were having our lunch, a stag started to roar away to the left of our deep little valley, and was almost immediately answered by a stag away to the right. After a few more roars, it became obvious that these stags were roaring at each other through the mist, and were coming towards each other's challenge. We did not know quite what would happen, where they would meet, or which would get our wind or, indeed, if they would cross our little glen out of sight, but we hastily put our sandwiches back in our pockets and stayed put to await events. The mist magnifies everything, including noise, but the noise of the roars was getting uncomfortably close. We were beginning to wonder what would happen and, afterwards, the wives admitted that they were getting quite alarmed. I took the rifle out of its cover, intending to hand it to my friend when I could make up my mind how he could get a shot. The stag on the left was getting very close, and the roars extremely loud. There was a lull on our right, and I feared that the stag had got the wind, possibly in an eddy. I stepped across the burn and took a step or two up the side to look when, suddenly, there was the most enormous roar and the stag, looking simply huge, appeared on the edge of the valley straight above me, and no more than 30ft (9m) away. I could not hand over the rifle, he would have seen the movement at such close range, and would have rapidly disappeared again. I took a quick look at his head and shot him through the neck straight from the shoulder, standing. He fell down stone dead, and I had to jump to get out of the way. I have been hit by a grouse that I have shot from a grouse butt, and had near misses from falling pheasants, but I have never been nearly killed by a falling stag before, and I do not expect to be again!

The other occasion which I remember was the last day of the season, when my host particularly wanted a stag to take home. The day, of course, turned out in the morning to be a day of mist almost right down, with little prospect of clearing. It had been arranged that my host should go out with the stalker himself on the home beat and I should go to the far beat with a man who had been brought up there, had acted as pony-man, had one year or so as stalker for someone else and, temporarily, had come back: the stalking was therefore to be rather a joint affair. As our orders were to get a stag if possible, we decided to try and stalk in the mist with the aid of my labrador. We sent the pony-man along a very well-marked pony track, with strict instructions to wait where a particular burn crossed it, which place he swore he knew, and we thought he could not miss it.

We went up the hill, seeing nothing until we got near the top, when we suddenly spotted a beast on the skyline, not far away. It was clearly a stag, but the horns were very small, though the beast looked very large in the mist: I was convinced it was a good knobber. The part-time stalker said I had better shoot it. He thought it must be a rather small switch because it looked so large. However, I continued my refusal to shoot it and, greatly to his credit, we did not fall out in any way over this. Soon, it moved on and we were able to pass fairly closely as we ourselves went on, when we did see, at close range, that it was in fact a knobber, although it had looked very large because of the mist.

We went over the top of the hill towards where I knew there to be a largish flat of peat hags, though we could not see them. The dog indicated that there were deer ahead, and we pushed on towards

the peat hags, soon hearing a stag roaring ahead of us where the dog
had been indicating. We went on carefully, trying to keep ourselves
as low as possible, in order to keep the ground in front of us on the
sky-line and ourselves off it. We reached the peat hags, when it was
clear from the occasional roar that the stag was driving his hinds
away from us through the hags. We hurried on, keeping low in the
tortuous gaps and channels through the hags, until the dog indicated
that the deer were close. We peered over the edge but could see
nothing but mist all around, and the ground for only a distance of
about 50yd (45m). We were just wondering what to do, when a loud
roar sounded out of the mist in front of us, and a second or so later
the vast shape of a stag and one hind appeared, coming towards us.
He was clearly chasing this errant hind, who had left the rest: she
might have heard something and come back to investigate, or might
have been merely asserting her independence, as hinds do, not
infrequently. There was not time to speculate, or to do more than
have a quick look to be sure he was not run and was, at least, in the
shootable class, and then he was dead the next moment he stopped,
and before he went back into the mist.

Having gralloched him, we now started to have trouble, since
the stalker-for-the-day, not having been on that hill for several
years, admitted he did not know where he was. I, fortunately, had
my compass (which I always carry) and knew these hags drained
down into the stream which crossed the pony path. We followed
the drainage direction of the peat hags and soon found a small
stream which, in turn, we followed. We deliberately left clear
foot-marks all the way in the peat, or built frequent small cairns
where foot-marks did not show clearly, so as to be sure of being
able to retrace our steps to collect the stag. In fact, we soon reached
the main stream, built a good cairn so as to see where to turn off on
our return, and set off down the stream to the pony path, where,
to our dismay, there was no pony or pony-man.

Had he got tired and, although told to wait, gone home; or had
he gone on? We were looking for tracks, when the dog again came
to our rescue, indicating clearly that he had gone on – somehow she
knew we were in trouble, and what it was, although there could
have been no apparent difficulty to her with her excellent scenting
powers. We followed her on up the path, and soon confirmed the
position by fresh pony tracks, though these were not so easy to

distinguish, as the pony had used that path a lot during the season. Pressing on hard, we finally caught up with the pony and man, who said he had heard the shot and was sure it was further on up the path (which it had not been) and so had gone on. It was pointless to argue, or to emphasize the dangers of getting lost on these occasions, beyond a few brief observations which the stalker made. We were at least 30 to 50 miles (50–80km) from any civilisation in any direction except that of the lodge.

We retraced our steps, loaded up the stag, and so home with the mission accomplished, which was all the more welcome because my host had failed to be so lucky and now had a stag to take home as required.

This was a memorable day and there was, in fact, no danger; but it serves to illustrate the care necessary on the hill in mist, how easy it is to get lost when things look quite different, and how wrong it is for pony-men, and others, to depart from the agreed plan; and also the advantages of a dog.

10

WEATHER FORECASTING
FOR THE HILL

Hollow laughter sounds at the statement that meteorology is not a precise science. Let us, however, examine the reasons for this, since the weather affects all our lives, and more than ever when stalking. Mist is the stalker's greatest enemy, so we will consider that in most detail.

The weather in this country is basically controlled by depressions and anticyclones. Scientists can say, up to a point, when conditions are favourable for the development of either of these systems but, so far, they have been unable to say exactly when or where they will develop. Similarly, since depressions and anticyclones move and, since they develop and decline, before meteorology can become a precise science, scientists need to be able to say for certain whether any particular depression or anticyclone will move in a certain direction, or will develop or decline and, until these three problems are solved by the physicists, meteorology is likely to remain an imprecise science.

This may help those who tend to pour scorn on the weather forecasters to understand the difficulties under which they operate. Their other great dilemma is that the British public insists, or the media think it does, on very brief weather forecasts to cover a very

Spying

large area and quite a long time. There are considerable variations in weather over short distances, especially in mountainous country, as every countryman will know, and it is very difficult to cover these variations in the short space of time or print available.

The stalker's problem is to apply the forecast to his particular area, and to be sufficiently aware of the principles on which the forecast is made to be able to correct for errors in it by observation of the current weather. The errors are frequently due to incorrect timing, when a depression hurries up or slows down, or when the wind increases or decreases due to a depression deepening or decreasing more rapidly than the forecaster thought likely. For this, it is almost essential to see the weather chart, that is to say, the one with fronts and isobars which appears on some weather forecasts on the television and in some papers. It is a measure of the ignorance which the media attribute to the British public that these charts are so comparatively rare.

The facts behind certain weather phenomena are basically simple and, as this is not the place for mathematical calculations, let us content ourselves with merely stating them. Air can absorb a certain amount of water in the form of water vapour which is in the gaseous state, and is entirely invisible in the air; the amount which it can absorb is dependent on the temperature; the hotter the air is the more it will absorb, provided it is available. This absorption goes on until what is called the saturation point is reached, when no more can be absorbed and, if exceeded, the excess water will condense out in the form of little droplets, so forming cloud or mist, and that is anything but transparent, of course. If the process continues in a cloud, the droplets will enlarge, and fall to the ground as rain, snow or hail.

The next most important point, therefore, is what causes the air to cool or to heat up. Contrary to the usual belief, the sun's rays pass almost entirely through the air forming our atmosphere (provided there is no cloud) and reach the surface of the earth, and it is only here that their heating effect is felt. In the absence of cloud during the daytime, the sun heats up the ground, then the air comes in contact with the ground and is itself heated up. As everyone knows, hot air rises because it is less dense and so what is known as a convectional air current of rising air over the hot ground is set up. At night, in the absence of the sun's rays, and cloud, the ground cools down, this in turn cools the air, and the reverse process is set up. In mountainous countries, this results in a draining of the cold air down the mountain sides which, if conditions are favourable, can give rise to what is known as a 'katabatic' wind, of which the most famous are the Mistral off the Alps in the South of France or, in this country, the Helm Wind in the Eden Valley.

Stalking last winter in the snow, I had a good example of the value of a little knowledge as set out in this chapter. The low afternoon sun did not reach the bottom of the glen and a party of hinds, with which there was one we wanted to shoot, had moved up a south-westerly-facing hill and were lying in the snow in the sun. The wind was very light south-west and the stalker, therefore, said we would have to go above the deer. We, therefore, went further down the glen and started to climb the hill; but when we got on to the face we found that the wind was blowing down it. The stalker said this must be an eddy and it probably would not hold where the deer were but I replied that it was a katabatic wind caused by the air getting cold in contact with the snow on the hillside and draining down the hill, and I thought it would hold where the deer were. We, therefore, came in below the deer and immediately to their south-west, that is to say, immediately downwind of what was the prevailing wind for that day, but the katabatic wind did, in fact, hold and, although we had to wait quite some time for the hind we wanted to get into a suitable position, we duly got our shot, whereas, if we had come in above them they would undoubtedly have got our wind.

The stalker, too, was quite right in his selection of hind for, although it was a very small hind, it proved to have its front incisor teeth worn right down to the gum and was geld both the year before and for the current year: we doubted whether it had ever had a calf.

To return to the weather, the other important thing to remember is that air cools when it expands, and heats up when it is compressed as, when one pumps up a bicycle tyre with a hand-pump, one finds the pump getting quite hot, due to the compression of the air in the pump. Pressure decreases with height and so, accordingly, when air rises it expands and cools; and when it subsides it is compressed by the increasing pressure, and warms up. The rate of cooling as air rises is about 5°F (3°C) per 1000ft (300m) (for the technical, that is known as dry adiabatic lapse rate). This drops to about 3°F (2°C) per 1000ft (300m) if the air is saturated so that, as it rises, water separates out as mist or cloud. The difference is due to the latent heat of vaporisation of the water, and that rate is known as the wet adiabatic lapse rate. When, therefore, the wind forces air over a hill, it forces it to rise, and so cool and, if it contains sufficient moisture, it will cool sufficiently for the moisture to separate out as cloud or mist, which is known as 'orographic' cloud or mist. This mist is a very frequent enemy of stalkers, who will be all too familiar with the days when damp air is blowing in from the sea. There is a lovely clear day down below, possibly where the lodge is, but as soon as one gets up the hill, one runs into cloud at, perhaps, 1000ft (300m). People will sit and say that this cloud or mist will disperse during the day, because it is clear out to sea, little realising that it is, in fact, forming all the time, as the air is forced up over the hill, and it will not disperse until conditions change, either through a shift of wind direction or by the air getting less damp for some reason (Diagram 1).

One often gets plumes of cloud forming on the lee side of the top of a high hill, where the height of the hill is such that the air cools to saturation point only at about the top. The famous 'Levanter' cloud which forms over the west side of the Rock of Gibralter in an east wind, and will be well-known to Service personnel who have served

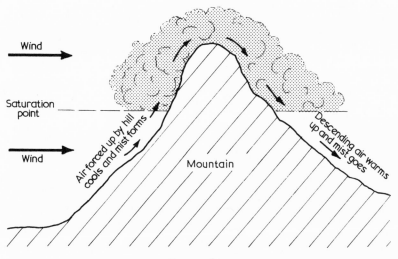

Wind

Saturation point

Wind

Air forced up by hill cools and mist forms

Mountain

Descending air warms up and mist goes

1 Orographic mist

there, is a good example of this. Here the air has had a long fetch over the warm Mediterranean and gets nearly saturated, so that the lift over the Rock cools it sufficiently to produce a cloud.

This, then, is orographic cloud or mist and, if one finds it forming on a day's stalking, there is very little point in waiting for it to clear unless one has good reason for supposing that the conditions, that is to say, the wind direction or the dampness of the air, will change during the day. If conditions remain the same, the mist will rise slightly as the sun's rays penetrate to a certain extent and warm up the ground, but this is only a very slow process, the general effect being for the cloud or mist to reflect the sun's rays and not let it through to heat the ground.

The next form of mist with which we have to contend is also explained by physics. As we have seen, the sun's rays warm the ground in daytime but, at night, the ground re-radiates the heat which it has received, and so it cools down. Both these processes are inhibited by cloud cover, because the cloud reflects the heat rays, either back out into the atmosphere in the daytime, or back to the ground at night.

However, on a clear night, the ground will cool, so the air in contact with it will cool and, if saturation point is passed, then mist will form. This is the standard morning or valley mist, which tends to collect in the valleys on still nights helped by the katabatic wind mentioned above (cold air draining into the valleys). This type of morning mist will clear during the day, because the reverse process will set in, and the ground will warm up, so warming the air and taking it back above saturation point, when it is able to re-absorb the moisture which had separated out in droplets. Under very still conditions, dew may form on the ground instead of mist in the air.

This kind of mist forms under still conditions, usually, because, if there is a wind, the turbulence produced mixes up the lower layers of the air much more, and so reduces the cooling effect.

It will have been noticed that no mention has been made so far of fronts: there are three types of front, a warm front, a cold front and an occlusion. When one mass of air, which is either warmer or colder than another mass of air, meets the latter, they do not immediately mix, but form only a thin mixing zone.

A warm front is when the following mass of air is warmer than the forward lot of air, and the warmer air tends to override the colder, forming a narrow mixing zone between the two air masses, which tends to slope upwards and forwards. Because of the mixing along the actual interaction of the two air masses, resulting in cooling of the warmer air in contact with the colder and because of the warm air rising up over the cold, cloud will form, and by the process continuing, then rain.

A cold front is the opposite. Here, the colder air is the following air and, being denser, it tends to undercut the warmer air ahead, so

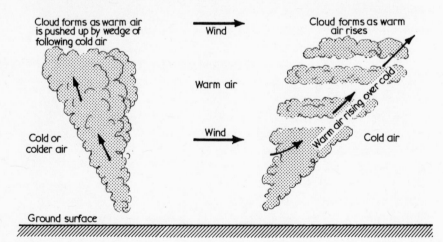

2   *Left*: cold front; *right*: warm front

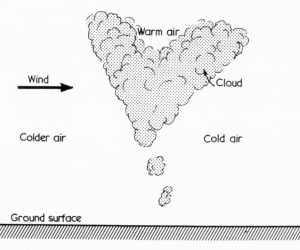

Wind

Warm air

Cloud

Colder air

Cold air

Ground surface

3 Occlusion—note the similarity between warm air rising over a hill (Diag 1) giving orographic cloud and warm air rising over cold (Diag 2) on a warm front giving frontal cloud

that the interaction between the two air masses is a plane sloping backwards with the colder air underneath again. It is along this mixing zone that cloud and rain will form. Again, the warm air is pushed up by the following cold air (Diagram 2).

Finally, an occlusion is a combination of a warm and a cold front, where the warm mass of air has been forced up off the surface altogether, so that one gets three mixing zones. Firstly, at a higher level, there is a zone corresponding to the original warm front and, behind that, a zone corresponding to the original cold front and, below the middle point of these the mixing zones, between the original first cold mass of air and the last cold mass of air which came along to form the cold front, a further front called an occlusion (Diagram 3).

This concept may be a little difficult to follow but, for practical purposes, it is not very material, except to remember that it is a combination of a warm and a cold front, and that, therefore, the cloud will be in front of, and behind, the central point.

As will be seen from the description of a warm front sloping upwards and forwards to the direction of the wind, in other words the direction of travel, the first indication will be high cloud and, equally, that will apply to an occlusion, where the upper part is, in fact, the warm front. This is followed by a gradual increase and lowering of layer-type clouds. These layer-type clouds of high and medium height are of great importance to a stalker in interpreting the weather forecasts, because the time of their arrival will tell him approximately whether or not the forecast which he has seen on the chart the night before is correctly timed, or whether it is running late or in advance.

On a warm front or occlusion, the cloud gradually lowers with the approach of the front, until extremely low cloud comes on a vigorous front, almost certainly accompanied by rain. The wind will back slightly as the front approaches and, with the actual passage of the front, will veer. That, of course, is of great importance to the stalker: it very often is quite pronounced and the passage of a front can fairly frequently be observed precisely.

A cold front is different, as mentioned above, because the mixing plane slopes backwards to the direction of travel. The slope is almost invariably more vertical than the slope of the warm front, and the clouds have a much more vertical formation than the truly layer-type clouds on a warm front. The onset of a cold front is much more abrupt; the bank of cloud can usually be seen approaching, but it does not go overhead like the high and medium cloud on a warm front. The wind backs in the same way as a warm front before the approach, and veers, often more sharply and to a greater extent, on the passage of the front.

In the case of an occlusion, warm air being all above, there will probably still be some high- or medium-layer cloud which will obscure the more vertical cloud on the cold front from ground observations.

If one is on the hill, therefore, ahead of a warm front, one may expect a period of low cloud and probably rain, which will clear fairly abruptly. A cold front is followed by a period of showery conditions but, in between the showers, visibility is usually good, the cold front producing showers more than continuous rain, because of the more vertical cloud formation.

The fronts form when a depression, originally started in one type of air, either warm or cold, moves into another type of air, and then a second air-mass gets sucked into the depression in the form of a wedge. Alternatively, the front itself, being a mixture zone between two different air-masses, is a very favourable place for a fresh depression (or, as it is sometimes called, a wave) to form:

then, of course, there are already the two air-masses present. Although one can say that a front is a place where a wave may form, the difficulty is estimating whether, in fact, it will form, and when.

However, using these principles, and observing the weather where one actually is, it is frequently possible to get a much more accurate picture of the weather for that day than that given in the forecast.

Most 24-hour forecasts go wrong, where they go wrong at all, through errors in timing, because a depression either does not take the expected track and turns one way or the other, or simply becomes stationary. Alternatively a depression may decrease or increase in vigour more quickly or more slowly than anticipated, though this latter facet has been reduced considerably by the advent of the excellent satellite pictures which are now available, and show, by means of the amount of cloud in a depression, the present activity of the depression – 48-hour and longer-range forecasts go wrong for the above reasons and, also, due to the formation of depressions which had not been foreseen.

It is, of course, quite impossible to write a whole treatise on meteorology in one chapter, but we have analysed and discussed, in a colloquial way, the stalker's main enemy, mist and fog. Other obvious things, such as convection showers and thunderstorms, have been omitted because, basically, these, although unpleasant, do not give rise to mist and fog and do not, therefore, interrupt stalking.

It has also been assumed that the reader knows a little about the subject, such as that depressions rotate anti-clockwise and anti-cyclones clockwise in the northern hemisphere; that the nearer together the isobars on the weather chart, the stronger the wind; that the wind blows nearly parallel to the isobars, but slightly across them, towards the lower pressure side; and that the stronger the wind, the faster the front will move. However, it may be as well to add that the front moves fastest when it is lying at right-angles to the wind, and the more trailing it is, that is to say, the more parallel to the isobars the front becomes, the slower it moves until, ultimately, it may be lying in the direction of the wind, in which case it becomes stationary.

We have also not mentioned land and sea breezes. These do affect coastal forests, but not to a great extent in Scotland, because there is seldom enough sun. A sea breeze, however, blows in the daytime, when the land gets heated up by the sun, and so heats the air above it, which rises, drawing in colder air from the sea. A land breeze blows at night, when the land cools down for the opposite reason, namely, that the land radiates heat and, therefore, the sea becomes the warmer, and it is the air over the sea that starts to rise, drawing air in from the colder land. This is often reinforced by a katabatic wind, when the land cools on the mountain sides near the sea in Scotland. If that wind is found to be blowing in the morning, it will, of course, decrease and ultimately reverse during the daytime.

Turbulence also has to be borne in mind; when wind blows over the ground, obstacles set up turbulence; the larger the obstacle the more the turbulence. This results in mixing of the lower layers of air, which may thus rise to the level where droplets of water form, so giving a layer of low cloud instead of what, apart from the effect of turbulence, would have been mist. Because of the increased mixing, what would only have been cloud may be turned into cloud and rain, or vice versa when the obstacles are small. Thus, removal of hedgerow trees on a large scale, as in East Anglia, results in less turbulence and less rainfall.

It must be remembered that local effects, such as katabatic winds, land and sea breezes, orographic fog and morning mist, all mentioned above, are superimposed on top of the weather pattern, whatever it may be, dictated by the presence or absence of depressions or anticyclones. That is to say, one must take account of both together; and that, in turn, is what accounts for local variations of weather, over often quite short distances.

II

A DAY ON THE HILL

So far, we have discussed the theory of stalking and the place of deer in the Highlands of Scotland, and have seen that, from every aspect, stalking is not only advantageous but is, indeed, a necessity, from the point of view of the ecology in general, and the preservation of our heritage in the countryside.

There are many books which give accounts of days stalking. I will not endeavour to emulate them, but a book on the subject would hardly be complete without some account of actual stalking, which I, therefore, give in these last two chapters, drawing attention, as far as possible, to the points made earlier.

The wind was moderate westerly and we, therefore, took the car up to the south-east corner of the forest, the easterly boundary of which was a burn running down a steep-sided corrie, rising to 3000ft (900m) on one side, and rather more on the other. We intended to go up this corrie, along the march. The burn is a large one, as Scottish burns go, and it must, in the ages past, have been much larger to have cut this deep corrie for some three miles between the hills on either side. Beyond, the land opened out into a flattish area of peat hags and small hummocks, before rising up again into a line of lower hills running east and west. No doubt, this area of peat hags

Very good young stag in prime and a good middle-aged hind

and flattish ground had, at some time past, been a large loch which provided the water for the burn, or river as it must have been then, to cut its cleft through the hills. A small loch still remains.

Because this corrie was the eastern march of the forest, and gave access to this high plateau beyond the first range of hills, stalkers had no doubt gone up it in the prevailing westerly or south-westerly winds for many years. There was a well-marked pony track all the way up the side of the burn, crossing where necessary and used, in fact, jointly by both the forest on the west of the burn and that on the east, as required by them respectively, according to the wind.

Our plan was to go up this pony track, getting a stalk, if we could, on our side of the burn and, if not, hoping for a stalk on the plateau beyond.

These steep corries are very difficult to stalk if the true wind is blowing at right angles to the corrie, as it was today. The reason for this is that the wind does not blow over the top of the hill, down the face into the corrie, and up the other side, but invariably eddies either up or down in the bottom of the corrie. Towards the top of the corrie, on the windward side, the wind tends to blow over the top of the hill and out into the air-space in the middle of the corrie, then to come round in a sort of roll or horizontal vortex, blowing, therefore, up the windward side of the corrie face about the middle. Finally, at the very top, there is an area where the wind does blow over the top and down to a certain extent.

The other side of the corrie, the wind will blow across the corrie high up, and up the face when it hits the face, but lower down, about the middle of the face, there will be an area where the wind, having hit the face, and no doubt being influenced by the roll or vortex in the middle of the corrie, blows down in the circulation of the roll.

Thus, the basic picture is of the wind blowing up the corrie or down the corrie along the lower layers; a roll in the middle causing the wind to blow down the middle of the leeward face and up the middle of the windward face; and, at the top, an area on the lee-ward face where the wind is blowing up and, on the windward face, an area where it is blowing down.

It will be appreciated that this is a most complicated picture and, just as the eddies behind a large rock in a river form and move on and then re-form, in what appears to be a haphazard fashion, so the eddies in the general air flow of the wind over a corrie like this keep changing, and moving on or up and down, making it extremely difficult to stalk.

I think, because of the continually changing wind direction under these conditions, deer become unsettled, and never favour this corrie very much, except under storm conditions when they can get shelter in the bottom or when there are very light winds and no eddies, the latter point confirming the fact that it is the continually changing wind-direction which the deer do not like.

We were able to spy the foothills of ground before the mouth of the corrie. We did not expect to see anything there, and did not, so we proceeded up this bit to the corrie in more or less open order, chatting or not as we felt inclined. One goes out to stalk, but also to enjoy oneself, so it is important that all the party should know roughly what is going on, how it is to be achieved, and what is

expected of each of them. There is no denying that, for a person
who knows the basis of stalking, it is very much easier to get deer if
one stalks alone; probably, for the very simple reason that the more
people there are, the easier it is for the deer to see them. But that
never seems to me to be a good reason for not sharing one's pleasure
with other people, or for refusing to take out on the hill people,
often wives, who do not want to shoot, although some wives are
very good shots.

Some professional stalkers are very much against taking out
anybody but the gentleman who will shoot: that attitude seems to
me to be either an admission of incompetence on the part of the
stalker (although an additional person or two may make it more
difficult to stalk, it also makes it correspondingly more sporting), or
an admission that they cannot or will not instruct the spectators
properly. Of course, there are limits on numbers, and stalking
parties over four or five carry the sporting aspect too much in
favour of the deer.

The rule, therefore, ought to be that, if people want to walk
over the hill and just do that, they ought to go and do it somewhere
where it does not interfere with stalking; but if they want to come
out stalking, then they should be sufficiently interested in the actual
stalking to find out and abide by the accepted practices.

Therefore, on this particular day, where the beginning part of the
day was merely, in effect, an open order walk on the hill, that was
quite acceptable; but when we reached the mouth of the corrie we
wanted to spy the corrie itself to see what deer lay ahead of us. At
that point, it is essential to let the stalker go in front, in case there
happen to be deer close, let him get over the hillock from which he
intends to spy the corrie and then follow him carefully and sit down
beside him in the heather on the back of the knoll. It is when
crossing into this position that the day's stalking proper may be said
to commence, and that is the point at which those members of the
party who have taken off their combat jackets or coats, so exposing
bright-coloured shirts, must put them on and be prepared to keep
them on for the remainder of the day until the stalk is completed,
whether or not the spy reveals any deer; but up to that point there
is no reason at all for getting unduly hot.

On this particular day, we spied the corrie carefully: one always
seems to spy one's own side first because any deer there are,

theoretically, of more interest than any in the neighbouring forest
on the other side of the corrie. But it is equally important to make
sure of what deer there may be on the other side, not because they
can be stalked but because they can very easily be moved by walking
up on our own side, or up the joint pony path and, if they start to
move, they will readily be seen by the deer on our side, and so
spoil the whole thing. Before, therefore, any plans can be made, it is
essential to know what deer are on both sides. In fact, in this
particular corrie, it is often much more difficult to get past deer on
the adjoining forest than it is to stalk deer on our own side, which is
rather rougher.

However, on this particular day, we could see nothing on our own
side, and on the other side only a party of stags high up the hill. As it
is three miles up the corrie, we could not spend too much time
crawling up the burn to get past the stags on the adjoining forest
without disturbing them and we, therefore, decided to go reasonably
slowly, keeping out of sight as much as we could while walking,
without resorting to crawling. We hoped that our spy had been
complete on our own side, but we knew that there were quite a
number of depressions which might have held deer, which would
have been invisible from where we had first spied. This is a risk
which one nearly always has to take when looking along a face.

It now became necessary to walk what, for want of a better word,
I may call 'properly': this consists of allowing the stalker to walk
first, which is an invariable rule in stalking, followed by the person
who is to have the shot, and then the spectators. It is essential that
the party should keep together behind one another, as close together
as practicable. I have never entirely satisfied myself why it should be
that a party proceeding like this should be less visible to deer than
where it is strung out, but much experience has convinced me that
it is so. I can only conjecture that, if one of the spectators lags
behind, he or she never stops when the rest of the party stops
(because they have seen deer, or because the deer are looking); or,
possibly, there is a larger area over which the people can be seen;
anyhow, it does not work, and it is essential to keep together and to
stop when the stalker stops. The stalker will realise that he has the
party behind him and, if he stops in such a position that one or more
of the people following will be on the skyline to the deer which he
has just seen, then he must get them down quickly, though any

actual movement should not be made fast. By this, I mean that he should signal the person or people concerned to come down to him, but they should come slowly, avoiding any fast movement, which deer always notice more than anything else.

We proceeded up the pony track like this, stopping at intervals to spy, as new pieces of ground came into view, but saw nothing more. Going at a steady but not fast pace, and keeping close together, we got past the stags above us on our right without their noticing. They were about half-a-mile (0.80km) away when we were immediately below them but, at this point, we kept along the burn side, on their side of the burn, so that the burn was our background: the movement of the water tends to obscure other movement. We were just congratulating ourselves that we had successfully completed this manoeuvre, (the less one moves deer the better, even if they are not on one's own ground) when two stags suddenly put their heads up and it was obvious that, although we had got quite a bit further away from them, they had now seen us. We sat down and waited for about ten minutes, when they put their heads down and commenced to graze again.

If it had been essential not to move them, we should have waited longer and should then have proceeded very carefully; but, in fact, the day was getting on and, as we were past them, it did not matter quite so much. We, therefore, resumed our walk, keeping close together and trying to avoid looking up at the stags too much, for it is faces that show up probably more than anything else, provided one is properly clad. However, having once seen us, they were on the alert and, very shortly after we had started to move, they picked us up again but, fortunately, started to move back and up the hill, which did not matter. It was, indeed, where they would not disturb any deer on our side, so we continued to the head of the corrie, checking each side corrie as it opened up, but finding nothing more.

As we neared the head of the corrie, we became more apprehensive, because the wind was still blowing strongly up the corrie on to the backs of our necks, and we hoped very much that there would be no deer just over the skyline, which was then no more than 300yd (275m) ahead. Both the stalker and I knew that the wind would be blowing in its true direction from the west, across the plateau. There is, however, an area where the two winds meet, the true westerly wind sweeping the eddy coming up the corrie away to the east; provided the main wind is steady, this area or strip where the two winds join often remains remarkably constant and narrow. By knowing the contours of the ground, one can usually work out exactly where it will be; and to somebody who knows a bit about stalking, but does not know the ground intimately, what seems a remarkable stalk can sometimes be achieved apparently downwind, when the deer are, in fact, just beyond the mixing zone of the two winds.

In our present case, the mixing zone was just about the skyline but, for a distance of about 50yd (45m) on either side of the skyline, there were eddies where the wind would go first one way then the other, and we hoped there were not deer in the 50yd (45m) over the skyline, or on the slope up to the right, where the true wind would carry the wind coming up the corrie, and our wind with it, up that slope.

We proceeded to keep as near our march as possible up the burn, and on to the skyline. Sure enough, about 50yd (45m) before the ridge, we began to notice the first puffs of wind in our faces, at times. Proceeding very cautiously, and spying at almost each step or, at any rate, the stalker keeping a very sharp eye out in front all the time, he finally spotted a hind's head about a quarter-of-a-mile (0.40km) away to our left, and up the northern slope of the hill, the other face of which had formed the western side of the corrie up which we had come. At that range, the deer were close and no risks could be taken, so that was the point at which the stalking party had to be left behind and the stalker crawled on for a bit up the burn to see what other deer there were with the hind whose head we had seen. He came back after a few minutes and reported that there were about eight hinds with a not very large stag, but quite definitely a switch, and a couple of small stags above. They were just over the ridge on the north face, but clearly in the true wind, which would be blowing along that face.

We decided to take the switch, although it was smallish, probably five or six years old (as indeed we confirmed when we shot it). We had agreed before starting out that my friend would take the first shot and then, if it should be possible to get a second stalk I would take that. The stalk itself would be easy, provided the wind behaved true to form and was not diverted as a result of some particularly violent eddy in the corrie. All we had to do was to cross the intervening head of the corrie below the skyline and then crawl up the ridge a bit until we came into sight below the deer. The danger point was the last bit, because the ridge was rather rounded and we should there be on the deer's skyline, which is always a tricky position. That is the sort of place where, if the party consists of more than the stalker and the person who is to shoot, the first two should go on, and the remainder should wait behind.

There was an added reason for some of the party, at least, waiting behind in this particular case, namely, that the ponies were following us up the corrie about half-an-hour behind, and we had to stop them before they came in sight of the deer. What we, therefore, planned was that the stalker and the rifle should go on, and the other three of us should wait. We would be able to see the stalkers getting on to the ridge, but would not be able to see the deer: that is a thing which must sometimes be accepted by spectators out stalking.

We arranged that we should wait until we saw them actually in the firing position and then, if no shot followed, we should very carefully crawl forward up the burn to where the stalker had gone to look at the deer originally, so that we could see a bit more. That would involve watching very carefully, and stopping immediately any deer showed any interest but, provided we did this carefully, it would do no harm, because the reason for no shot being taken at once would be almost certainly that the stag was lying down and in an awkward position: any slight uneasiness among the deer would probably get him on his feet. If a stag has to be got up, it is much better that this should be done by somebody at a distance rather than the person in the firing position but, even so, it has to be done very carefully, so that only a slight interest is aroused and no more.

The rut had only just begun and this young stag was not really rutting properly, which was why we had not heard him roaring. If rutting properly, stags do not lie for long, and steps to get them up should be avoided, because they are by no means always successful, even if executed with the greatest care, stags being capable of getting up and going off almost in one, without presenting a decent shot.

This day, we watched the stalker and rifle get on to the ridge and crawl carefully up it, noticing, incidentally, as they did this, how my friend (although crawling with the greatest care and keeping his body flat as told) waved his feet in the air from time to time. This is a common fault among those unused to crawling: for some reason, there is a tendency when crawling on one's stomach and pushing oneself along with the knees, to bend them and get one's feet in the air. I suppose one gets a better push but it has frightened many deer and is always a point to watch. However, on this occasion all was well, and we saw them getting into what was clearly the firing position, but no shot followed. As planned, we waited a bit, and then began to crawl up the burn until we were in sight of the deer and saw that, indeed, they were nearly all lying down, with the stag lying facing downhill, almost directly towards the stalkers. The deer had not picked us up, so we waited a bit, hoping the stag, perhaps, might change position and give a shot in so doing, but it was the middle of the day, a time when deer tend to lie down and chew the cud, as these were doing.

Nice as it is to sit and watch them on a day which is not too cold, I felt that something had to be done, both because there was the danger of a freak gust of wind so near where the two winds met, which would have put the deer off straight away and, probably, given no chance of a shot, and because the ponies were rapidly catching up, and somebody would anyhow have to go back to stop them, the pony-man having been told to wait on the ridge, where he could see the plateau. The obvious thing to do was to leave the remainder of the party sitting where they were and arouse the curiosity of the deer myself. This is best done by moving very cautiously, so that the deer do not see much, and moving away from them at the same time because, not unnaturally, deer are less afraid of something which is moving away from them. However, one has to do this in such a way that one can watch the deer as well. One has to move, therefore, so that one can look backwards at the deer all the time. I started, therefore, to crawl out of the burn up the other side at an angle, so that I could watch the deer and, sure enough, as soon as I had gone some yards out of the burn, one of the hinds started looking intently at me. I stopped at once, but she had clearly seen something and, after watching for a bit, got up to have a better look; that put several of the other hinds up, but the stag stayed lying where he was. I kept very still, fearing I had done the wrong thing and that the deer would be off in a rush. However, finally, the stag, wondering what it was all about, got up and stood looking about but facing directly towards the stalkers. After what seemed an age, he finally turned slowly, and with great relief I heard the crack of the rifle and the distinctive thud of the bullet striking home in the right place. He careered down the hill and collapsed, after about 50yd (45m), quite dead.

That was all just in time, because the ponies were nearly up. It was lunch-time, too, and we had our stag with a good shot and had all seen the stalk and, indeed, taken part in it, showing that even the spectators can co-operate if they know what is going on. The thing at this point, however, was to remember that we had had no opportunity of spying the plateau in front of us : fortunately, the stalker and I did both remember. Had we jumped up after the shot, not only would we have pushed the remainder of the deer off much too fast, which might have taken other deer with them, but we might easily have been seen by other deer further out on the plateau, and so spoilt the afternoon's stalking, which we intended to have.

As it was, the single shot frightened the deer very little; they often do not know really what one single shot is; and they moved off quite fast for a few hundred yards up the hill, and then slowed down and went fairly slowly over the top so, in fact, not taking other deer away with them. We, from our respective positions, spied the remainder of the ground in front of us, which was quite a large area, but there was nothing close, though several lots of deer on the far side. The spectator party retreated to where the ponies had by now arrived, just behind us, and the stalker and the rifle went to perform the necessary rites on the stag, and then came back to us.

We had seen deer on the opposite face across the plateau on both sides, so we had a hasty lunch and went up on to the ridge again, from where the shot had been taken, to have a good spy and see what the stags were like. The hill up the eastern side of which we had come, and on the north-eastern shoulder of which we now were, though low compared to the top, had a concave semi-circular face coming round and out again on the far side of the plateau beyond us. There was then a corrie through which another stream ran in a westerly direction and then, round the other side of the plateau, the line of hills which we had seen before. There were two lots of deer on this line of hills, and one lot on the semi-circular face of the hill on which we were but at the other side of the plateau, on a steep grassy slope. These proved to consist of about twelve hinds with an old six-pointer but heavy stag, which we could now hear roaring and see rounding up the hinds and driving off a small bunch of stags above him. Of the two lots on the other side, one had a nice stag with cups on the top, though we could not see whether he had double brows or not but, certainly, he was not one we would wish to shoot. The other lot was a party of younger stags which had not broken out at all, that is to say, they were still in their summer stag group and had not separated to look for hinds. There would, undoubtedly, have been one among this group which we could have shot in the proper process of culling but we could see no way of getting past the lot of hinds with the good stag and, even if we had got past them, we would have given them our wind before we could have got a shot at the bunch of stags.

We were, therefore, left with the old six-pointer and its hinds high up on the green face. This was an awkward place to stalk, because the face was concave, and we could not get along it on a level with them. The deer had a commanding view of the plateau, with its peat hags and, therefore, we could not work our way through the peat hags towards them and, even if we had succeeded in this, we would still have been too far off the deer when the peat hags merged into a gentle slope up to the bottom of the steep, green face. We could not go round and come in above them, because that was upwind from them: this would have been an easy approach but for the wind.

One cannot, however, always expect easy stalks and, sometimes, luck holds on what, at first, appears a near impossible one. We, therefore, decided to go for the six-pointer and to leave the ponies where we were, near the first stag, and where the pony-man could see across to the green face, giving him instructions that, if we signalled from there, he was to come across above the peat hags on the hard ground. We, ourselves, went higher up, with the intention of going round the top out of sight of the deer as far as the wind would let us, and then down a burn which would take us to the bottom of the green face but about 600yd (500m) from the deer.

It was lucky that the first lot of deer had gone away comparatively quietly and over the top for, had they gone through the face straight upwind, as they might well have done, they would have taken this lot of deer with them, thus confirming the wisdom of not frightening deer after one shot, even if successful.

We had no difficulty in climbing up the face and going along the

top and down our chosen burn though, in doing so, we probably
walked another two miles (3km), and climbed and came down
1000ft (300m). At the bottom, the burn ran out from its little gully,
and gave no cover across the open stretch below the green face.
When we got there, we came round the corner carefully, and could
see the whole of the green face stretching out in front and above us,
and the deer still well up it and 500yd (450m) away from us.

The hinds seemed to want to make up the face, and we hoped
they would, when we could easily have followed them and caught
them on the top over the ridge. However, the stag kept rounding
them up and driving them back down, because of the presence of
the other small stags up at the top. He should, of course, have gone
up and driven the other stags off but he did not seem to know the
'rules'! We sat for a bit in this position, unable to go on, and hoping
that the deer would move over the top in spite of the stag's efforts.
But the day was by now getting on, and we had still to go back and
load one stag, so we decided to try a stalk and, if it failed, well, we
had had a very pleasant day. This was obviously a situation where a
long, flat crawl would be necessary, and the fewer people to attempt
it the better, so we had to leave the spectator party behind to watch
the proceedings. They would be able to see both the deer and our
crawl from the corner.

The stalker and I set off to creep, absolutely flat, round the
bottom of the face, which gave a little, but very little, cover,
mainly because the grass was a bit longer there. We hoped to get
more or less below the deer, and then to find some little hump on
the face which we had failed to see so far, which would give us
enough cover to get, perhaps, half-way up. We both realised that all
this was tinged with more than a touch of optimism.

We proceeded, keeping as flat as possible, by the stalker crawling
10 or 15yd (10 to 15m), while I watched the deer carefully. He then
stopped and watched the deer, ready to signal me to stop immediately any looked suspicious. By this means, and at a very slow
speed, we got to very nearly below the deer, which were then about
350yd (320m) above us. There was not a single hump, as far as we
could see, to provide any cover up that face. I refused to take a shot
at that range, as a matter of principle, mainly, but also because an
uphill shot is always difficult. We lay for a bit, hoping for some
developments in our favour, but the position did not change. The

hinds kept wanting to go up but the stag kept wanting to drive them down, and in the end they stayed put, more or less.

At last, we decided that something must be tried and that the best chance was for me to crawl on very slowly, alone, watching the stalker all the time, who would in turn watch the deer and give me a signal immediately any of them showed signs of spotting me. I wriggled on slowly, avoiding any jerky movement and pushing the rifle in front of me, watching both the deer and the stalker, but mainly the latter. I had reduced the distance to under 300yd (275m) when, greatly to my surprise, one of the hinds suddenly decided to come down the hill towards me. There was a very small tussock in front of me which would make a good rest to shoot off, though it was not large enough to give cover and, anyway, it was only a yard or two (1 to 2m) in front of me. I, therefore, carefully wriggled on to this and got ready, the hind coming down to within about 120yd (110m) of where I was.

I wondered what best to do. If the hind saw me and did not go off too fast, the other deer might stand at the top and, if the stag presented a good target, I thought I might take a shot at that range: though, in the end, I probably would not have taken it, because I do not like long shots, even though I would be fairly confident of getting it, as I had a good rest and would be steady. I put the rifle on safe in front of me, and waited. I hardly dared to breathe as the hind came slowly on. I knew that, if only she would stop or go back a little, the stag would eventually come down and round her up: he was roaring at intervals and rounding up the other hinds, but seemed to have no interest in this one hind. However, he did finally look down the hill towards her and, when he did so, I heard a roar below and to my left, and realised the stalker was roaring at him gently. He stood and looked in great surprise, as well he might, and then started to trot down the hill towards the hind, giving a roar every 20yd (18m) or so, which the stalker answered. I am not sure whether the hind was a bit suspicious of the stalker's roars, or whether it was her lord and master trotting down the hill that made her think she should go back to the herd, but she turned and started to go back up the hill though, fortunately, not very fast. The stag on the other hand, encouraged by the stalker's roars, or perhaps infuriated is more accurate, came down towards the hind and me quite fast and, when he got just below where she was, he turned broadside on to drive her up the hill, back to his harem and away from his supposed rival. He was only just over 150yd (140m) off then, but was doing it all at a trot, except when he stopped to roar. However, the stalker knew what to do, and gave one of the little grunts that stags give in between roars; the stag stopped to have one last look, and it was, indeed, his last, for he gave an easy shot, broadside on as he was.

The stalk showed again the value of co-operation, for the crawl would have been impossibe without the benefit of the stalker watching the deer through his binoculars, and his superb knowledge of deer which enabled him to sense when the hind was going to see me before she really had, as well as his knowledge of when, and how much, or how little, to roar.

So ended a day when the gods of stalking seemed to be with us. We signalled up the ponies, loaded the stag and then picked up and loaded the other one on the way home and back down the pony track.

The reader may wonder why, earlier on, I described the wind as blowing up the eastern face of the hill in the corrie, whereas clearly, from the above description, it blew down this steep face, although both faces lay approximately north and south at right angles to the wind. The answer to that is that, in the first case, there was the steep corrie which helped the formation of a vortex in the middle and, as stalkers often put it, 'bounced the wind back'; whereas, in the second case, there was, below the hill, the large plateau of peat hags, across which the westerly wind blew evenly, so tending to assist the wind down the green face rather than cause a vortex.

A WASTED DAY, OR WAS IT?

We have discussed the nature and habits of deer, together with the principles involved in stalking, and we have seen how, oddly enough, the well-being of the deer herds is intimately bound up with stalking, so that it will be appreciated that there is a lot of pleasure and satisfaction to be got out of stalking properly. The shot itself is of little interest to the stalker, save to be quite sure that it kills the required beast cleanly and immediately. I, for one, am just as happy, in fact probably happier, to stalk for somebody else and watch him shoot the stag correctly, as I am to do it myself.

However, it should not be thought that this is the beginning and end of stalking. There is a great deal of pleasure to be had from being on the hill in the wild conditions which prevail and seeing nature at work in these circumstances.

I always look back on one particular day, which produced no stag but a great deal of interest, and I, therefore, recount this to illustrate the enjoyment to be had from merely being on the hill.

The forest was approximately square, the sides lying north and south, and east and west, with access to be had from the road running along the southern side and from a subsidiary road along the western side. The wind was south-south-west. We, therefore, decided to take the Land Rover, with the pony in a horse box, up to the north-west corner; here, we unboxed the pony and saddled it with its deer saddle. Fortunately, the river which forms the march was low enough to take the Land Rover across (without the horse-box), so the stalking party were able to get across dry-shod. The pony forded the river and we assembled on the far bank.

On the way up the road, we had already spied the steep face, up which we now had to go from the Land Rover, several times, but there was nothing to be seen on it, so we set off up it knowing that it would be very unlikely that we should see anything until we got into the saddle which we were making for at the top of the face. Even so, in the rutting season, one must always be prepared for a travelling stag to appear in the most unexpected places. We reached the saddle without incident, members of the party arriving at rather different times because the climb is very steep and, though the fitter members of the party can go at a reasonable walking speed, the less fit take longer! When one is actually stalking, it is of vital impor-tance that the party should keep together, but many stalkers forget that different people in different stages of fitness take different times to get up the initial climb which so often precedes a stalk. It makes for the pleasure of everyone if all arrive at the top in good order, it being far better to have this, and for the fitter people to wait at the top at a point where they can either spy the ground ahead or sit down just before that point until the others catch up.

The climb itself I always enjoy for, as one gets higher, one looks down at the valley below into wilder and wilder country, often almost on top of a buzzard or raven flying below. The pony, who is a great character, and knows perfectly well that he will have to go on, protests as we go up the hill, marking his disapproval by standing still, deaf to all entreaties and urgings of the pony-man leading him. He backs down the hill so that the pony-man cannot get behind him to push him on until, ultimately, the stalker is forced to come down from the head of the party and make to give the pony a good wallop from the back, at which point, before receiving the wallop which he knows he will get, the pony starts off at a great pace up the hill, almost dragging the pony-man after him. This the regulars have all seen before, but the pony insists on his joke each time.

So we reached the saddle, and sat down and spied carefully in the glen ahead, expecting, particularly, to see deer on the right-hand side at the back of the steep hill, which we had come up because that was sheltered from the wind. However, there were none; perhaps, the wind was funnelling too much up the glen and along the side of the hill. We continued along the stream which forms the march for the next half-mile (0·8okm), and then we branched off to the left up another hill beside a tributary burn which itself becomes the march. We spied at intervals, as each new bit of country opened up, until we reached the ridge or water-shed which forms the northern march. From here, we could spy down into a wide glen running up along into the main part of the forest and on to the ground beyond, and we got a wonderful panoramic view of the peaks for miles around. It is exhilarating but awesome to know that, if one set off from here in the wrong direction, either north or east or any way between these two points of the compass, one would have to walk between 30 and 50 miles (50 to 80km) in a straight line before coming to any road or habitation; and it is easy enough to set off in the wrong direction in mist or snow if one is not very careful!

We spied the corrie going up to the right. There was below us a good stag with about 15 hinds which he was holding against 5 or 6 small stags, which were alternately lying down and getting up, and walking about restlessly just out of his range. We sat and looked at the deer for some time, discussing the merits of the stag, which was a good, young ten-pointer (and, therefore, not to be shot) and the other stags, which included a small switch about three or four years old and a one-horned stag, slightly younger. Either of these would have been suitable. The switch might, possibly, have grown some points in later life but never a good head if there were no signs of points at four or even three. The one-horned stag we looked at more carefully because it might easily have been that he had broken the horn off at the coronet: even with the telescope we could see no sign of a coronet, however and, in any case, if he had broken it off, it probably would have damaged the coronet and so he would never have grown another horn, or another good horn, on that side.

The deer were about ½ to ¾ of a mile (0.80 to 1.20km) away from us, with the wind blowing almost from them to us, where we were on the ridge, but we suspected that it would funnel considerably up the corrie below, so that a stalk would have to be undertaken down the corrie. We could not go straight towards them, for the face was too open and they were well out into the corrie and would have a good view of that ground. We, therefore, decided to leave them and to go on along the watershed where, because the top here was very rounded, we would be out of sight of them, see what was in the head of the corrie and in another corrie stretching the other way beyond, and then come back to these deer, if we had not got one further on. The young stags were not large enough to do any harm this year, even if we did not get them. If we had gone down to stalk them, the wind funnelling up the corrie would have put anything out that was beyond. As has been mentioned before, it is of the utmost importance on the smaller forests not to put deer out of the forest on one day's stalking, or one will spoil the next.

All this we discussed as we sat and spied, watching at the same time an eagle quartering the ridge beyond for ptarmigan. Finally, he found a good covey and swooped towards them, when they took off with incredible speed, flying very fast, hugging the rocks below us and passing quite close, with the eagle in hot pursuit. The ptarmigan passed out of sight round a steep rocky face, the eagle following hard behind on half-closed wings. I have never seen an eagle take a bird on the wing, so I do not know what his intentions were – we never saw the end of the chase.

We went back to where we had left the pony out of sight on the watershed and continued on our way along it. We spied, as we went, but saw nothing more, and decided to keep right along the top until we had got to more or less the north-east corner of the forest, when we would work our way back down the face and down the big corrie, if necessary, to the deer we had seen originally.

After going about ¾ of a mile (1.20km), we saw ahead of us the ears of a deer appearing on the skyline. We sat down immediately but there was, of course, no way of hiding the pony, which stuck out like a traditional sore thumb on the bare hill-top. The deer continued towards us and then, greatly to our surprise, we realised that it was a this-year's calf, still with the vestiges of spots visible. It is very rare indeed to see a calf alone on the hill: this one seemed to be quite all right, however, and trotted on roughly towards us. When it was about 300yd (275m) away, it altered course slightly to come directly towards us, and increased speed. We watched it with much pleasure and interest, wondering what on earth it was doing, until we realised that it must have seen the pony and thought it must be another deer. It came right on at a good trot towards us, until it was about 120yd (110m) off, the pony being another 30yd (25m) behind us, when it stopped dead and looked at us for a long time. One could almost see the incredulity in its eyes as it looked from us to the pony and back again, wondering what we were and what we were doing on the hill. Fortunately, the wind was blowing across, so it did not get our wind, and it clearly had not the least idea what we were, still less that we were dangerous, or might have been! Finally, after staring at us for what seemed a long time, it started to walk back and forth slowly, with the peculiar stiff walk which deer exhibit when they are apprehensive but uncertain. All we wanted to do was to put it off in the direction of its mother, but that we did not know. We decided we were wasting too much time, and we would have to put it off somewhere, hoping it would go by some instinct towards its mother. So we stood up, and after we had done quite a bit of gesticulating and walking about, which only produced more indecision in the calf, it finally decided we were not the usual thing to find on the hill and went off at quite a sharp speed down into the corrie which we were going to stalk and where we ultimately discovered there was another herd of deer, with which it clearly joined up.

We were very glad we had come along just then and that the eagle had gone on in pursuit of its ptarmigan for, though they do not usually take three- or four-month-old deer calves, they would be very apt to have a go at one they found on its own. I have once seen an eagle persistently stooping on a young deer, in this case a yearling, and with each stoop driving it nearer and nearer to some precipitous rocks. The stalker who I was with on that occasion said that eagles would do this, ultimately getting the deer so confused that they were able to drive it over the rocks, where they hoped it would break a leg or injure itself in some way, thereby providing the eagle with a good meal.

It had been warm coming up the hill but now we noticed that the wind had veered south-west, bringing with it damper air from the sea and more cloud; probably, the air temperature was higher, but it felt cold with the wind and damp: clearly, a weak warm front had passed. We could see wisps of mist forming already on the top in front of us, so we hurried on, in order to get a spy into the far corrie before the mist came down altogether. There are times in stalking when one must hurry, but the actual stalk in to the deer should never be hurried, except as a last resort when deer are moving, or for some other very special reason.

We pushed on along the ridge and over the top in the mist, and were lucky enough to get a clearance shortly after, when we were able to spy the far corrie, seeing two lots of deer, each with a stag, and some outlying stags. The higher lot, which consisted of about ten hinds and an old six-pointer stag which would clearly never improve (and was, therefore, shootable), was on the shoulder between the far corrie and the big corrie up the top of which we had come. In other words, we had come along the ridge above this lot of deer without being able to see them. The lower lot consisted of rather more hinds with an eight-pointer stag of no great merit, but one which, if mated with a good hind, would probably produce a good stag, though the exact role of each parent in the production of a good stag is not entirely clear yet. However, it was obvious that, in these circumstances, we should give the eight-pointer the benefit of the doubt and go for the six-pointer. The deer were very restless, partly due to the stags' efforts to keep their respective lots of hinds separate as well as to keep the small stags off and partly, no doubt, due to the change in weather and shift of the wind.

Lunch-time was well past really, and we were just debating whether to have lunch or start our stalk when the matter was settled for us by the mist coming down again. So we had our lunch, a cold and damp affair, as it so often is, in the mist, which we hoped would clear again shortly. We could see it was patchy, from odd breaks, but it did not clear really well and we, therefore, decided to try and get lower and work along the face towards the six-pointer in the mist. The objection to doing this was that we might well be in an open space just when the mist cleared, if it did, and then we would be in a position when we could go neither forward nor backward without the deer's seeing. However, as the afternoon was now getting on, we decided we should take this risk.

Many people think that deer see much better than humans through the mist but, from my own experience, that is probably only marginally so. There is a great deal of luck about it in that what is really visible through the mist is movement, or an object on the skyline. Move one must and, if one is uncertain where the deer are, one is equally uncertain whether one comes over a small knoll on the skyline and that is just where the deer see one. However, on this occasion, we had some advantage because, although they were not roaring hard, both stags were roaring now and again. We could tell from this that they were still roughly where we had seen them, though the bottom lot were moving along. The wind was blowing across and up the hill, and we were about the middle of the face, with the deer we were trying to stalk slightly above us, so that we felt we must not, on any account, go on beyond them or they would get our wind. When we judged from the occasional roar that we were 300 to 400yd (275 to 350m) short of them, we decided we must wait for another clearance in the mist before making our final approach, and we sat down, taking such shelter as we could in a peat hag.

We had not sat more than ten minutes or a quarter-of-an-hour before the stalker nudged me and pointed along the hill below us, where the mist was rather thinner, and I saw coming along towards us, but rather beneath us, a fox. I knew that the stalker was itching to shoot him, for foxes do a lot of damage to lambs as well as deer

'. . . the stalker made a squealing noise. The fox at once looked up . . .'

calves on the hill, and among stalkers there is a great 'cachet' attached to each fox shot, and great competition as to who can shoot the
most. However, I was very anxious that my friend who was with us
should get a shot that day, for he was only staying for two or three
days, so I whispered that we could not disturb the deer. The fox came
on, running 10 or 20yd (10 to 20m), or perhaps a little more, and
then stopping to look about him. He passed about 120yd (110m)
below us and then turned out into the corrie, shortly disappearing
into a burn. He came out of the dip about 50yd (45m) on, standing a
long while there and looking around him, at which point he was
about 200yd (180m) off. I do not know what made him stand so long
there, except that I think it was probably where the other lot of deer
had crossed. Finally, he went on, doing short trots and stopping to
sniff and look around at frequent intervals.

We had been so intent on watching the fox and his antics that we
had hardly noticed the silence, but we suddenly realised that we no
longer heard the stag roaring in front of us. At that moment, the
mist suddenly lifted and the wind veered again (indicating the
passage of a weak cold front, as readers of Chapter 10 will realize),
and we were able to see well ahead of us: there were no deer
anywhere in sight. I whispered to the stalker 'I am sorry I couldn't
let you have a shot at the fox when he was below us, but I wanted my
friend to get a stag'. He whispered 'Keep quite still' and slowly slid
the rifle out of the cover. I said 'You cannot shoot it at that range',
to which he replied 'Keep quite still', and started making a little
squealing noise. The fox, although now nearly a quarter-of-a-mile
(0.40km) off, at once looked up: the stalker made a small squeal
again, and the fox turned round and came trotting towards us. Each
time he stopped, at about 50yd (45m) intervals, the stalker gave
another little squeal, so small that, sitting almost next to him and
having quite some difficulty in hearing him in the wind, which was
by then fairly strong, I could not imagine how the fox could possibly
hear that high-pitched little squeal, but he clearly did. He came
back, following the tracks that he had gone out on, even to going
into the burn, down which he had gone at the same place. When he
was in the burn and out of sight, the stalker got into firing position
with the rifle and, sure enough, very soon the fox's head appeared
out of the burn where he had gone in on his way down the face. The
stalker gave one more little squeal and the fox trotted another short

distance towards us, stopped again looking about him, and that was his last stop for, as soon as he turned broadside, the stalker got him straight through the heart at about a 150yd (140m) range.

The stalker went down to cut off his brush and I went back to bring on the pony which we had left behind. We re-assembled and went on to see if we could catch up with our deer. I had never heard a fox called like this before, and I asked the stalker what the call was, to which he repled that it represented a hare in distress. This, the fox clearly thought it was, but how it heard it at such long range I still do not know, though the stalker assured me he had done it often before and, since then, I have seen him do it again.

A single shot does not usually move deer very much if they have not seen, heard or smelt anything else, so we quite expected to find our deer when we got round the shoulder. In fact, we did find them, but both lots had joined up together, the bottom lot having come up the hill, and they were moving on in front of us, feeding rapidly. On looking back at it, I think there must have been a stray hind or knobber, which we had not seen in our quick spy while the mist was broken, which had run down and moved the bottom lot on, and they, in turn, had moved the top lot, and both lots had joined. We went on after them, but moving deer are very difficult to stalk and, finally, I sent the stalker and my friend on to see what they could do and went back to stop the pony and then bring him on, on the right track. My friend did, finally, get a shot but it was a long shot and rather hurried, as the stag was standing briefly on the skyline, but it was a clean miss. In hurrying, they had moved the deer we had originally seen in the bottom of the corrie southwards, towards where we wanted them for the following day, further into the forest and there was, therefore, nothing left to do, as the day was getting on, but to make tracks for home.

We carried on along the face and back the way we had come up, through the saddle and down to the waiting Land Rover. There was nothing on the pony: we had had one long and difficult shot, a shot which probably should not have been taken and, certainly, would not have been earlier in the day, though, provided one shoots so as to be sure either of a kill or a clean miss, a longish shot at the end of the day is just permissible.

I wondered idly, as we walked down the final steep slope, whether it was a wasted day. We had seen a great deal of nature on the high hills, which gave us much pleasure and, after all, one is very fond of the deer and, if they win sometimes, it adds a lot to the enjoyment. Stalking, like salmon-fishing, would never be worth it in terms of pleasure if the quarry did not have his successes too: long may it remain so.

ACKNOWLEDGEMENTS

Some of the information set out in this book was originally con-
tained in articles by me in *The Field* a few years ago, and I am very
grateful to the Editor for allowing me to reproduce it again. I am
also grateful to Dr Iain Colquhoun for his invaluable assistance and
for allowing me to reproduce parts of his thesis as set out in
Chapters 1 and 4, as well as Mrs Maxwell for the drawings, and to a
great many stalkers, family and friends, too numerous to mention,
for their assistance on so many occasions over many years.

BALLISTIC TABLE – 'NORMA' AMMUNITION

Line of sights 1½" above centre of bore.
+Indicates point of impact in inches above sighting point
−Indicates point of impact in inches below sighting point

Calibre Bullet weight Prod no	Velocity—Feet per sec				Energy—Foot pounds				Sight at yards	100 yards	200 yards	300 yards
	Muzzle	100 yards	200 yards	300 yards	Muzzle	100 yards	200 yards	300 yards				
243 Win. 100 gr/6.5 g 16002	3070	2790	2540	2320	2090	1730	1430	1190	100	0	−2.9	−10.6
									180	+1.1	−0.7	−7.4
									200	+1.4	0	−6.3
243 Win. 100 gr/6.5 g 16003	3070	2790	2540	2320	2090	1730	1430	1190	100	0	−2.9	−10.6
									180	+1.1	−0.7	−7.4
									200	+1.4	0	−6.3
6.5 Jap. 139 gr/9.0 g 16531	2430	2280	2130	1990	1820	1605	1401	1223	100	0	−5.4	−18.8
									130	+0.6	−4.1	−16.9
									200	+2.7	0	−10.8
6.5 Jap. 156 gr/10.1 g 16532	2065	1871	1692	1529	1481	1213	992	810	100	0	−8.5	−29.2
									130	+1.1	−6.3	−26.0
									200	+4.3	0	−16.4
6.5 Carcano 139 gr/9 g 16536	2576	2379	2192	2012	2046	1745	1481	1249	100	0	−4.7	−16.6
									180	+1.8	−1.1	−11.3
									200	+2.3	0	−9.6
6.5 Carcano 156 gr/10.1 g 16535	2430	2208	2000	1800	2046	1689	1386	1123	100	0	−5.7	−20.2
									180	+2.2	−1.3	−13.7
									200	+2.9	0	−11.7
6.5x55 77 gr/5.0 g 16550	2725	2362	2030	1811	1271	956	706	562	100	0	−4.8	−18.1
									180	+1.8	−1.2	−12.7
									200	+2.4	0	−10.9
6.5x55 80 gr/5.2 g 16528	3002	2398	1886	1499	1604	1023	633	400	100	0	−4.7	−19.3
									180	+1.7	−1.2	−14.2
									200	+2.3	0	−12.3
6.5x55 139 gr/9.0 g 16551	2854	2691	2533	2370	2512	2233	1978	1732	100	0	−2.3	−12.3
									180	+1.3	−0.8	−8.6
									200	+1.7	0	−7.4
6.5x55 139 gr/9.0 g 16557	2790	2630	2470	2320	2402	2136	1883	1662	100	0	−3.7	−13.3
									180	+1.4	−0.9	−9.2
									200	+1.8	0	−7.8
6.5x55 156 gr/10.1 g 16552	2495	2271	2062	1867	2153	1787	1473	1208	100	0	−5.3	−18.8
									180	+2.0	−1.3	−12.7
									200	+2.6	0	−10.9
270 Win. 130 gr/8.4 g 16902	3140	2884	2639	2404	2847	2401	2011	1669	100	0	−4.1	−10.7
									180	+1.0	−0.7	−7.7
									200	+1.4	0	−6.6
270 Win. 150 gr/9.7 g 16903	2800	2616	2436	2262	2616	2280	1977	1705	100	0	−3.6	−13.1
									180	+1.4	−0.9	−9.0
									200	+1.8	0	−7.7

Cartridge										Range			
7x57 150 gr/9.7 g 17002	2755	2539	2331	2133	2530	2148	1810	1516		100	0	−3.9	−14.3
										180	+1.5	−1.0	−9.8
										200	+2.0	0	−8.4
7x57 R 150 gr/9.7 g 17005	2690	2476	2270	2077	2411	2042	1717	1437		100	0	−4.2	−15.2
										180	+1.6	−1.0	−10.4
										200	+2.1	0	−8.9
7x57 R 150 gr/9.7 g 17006	2690	2476	2270	2077	2411	2042	1717	1437		100	0	−4.2	−15.2
										180	+1.6	−1.0	−10.4
										200	+2.1	0	−8.9
7 mm Rem.M 150 gr/9.7 g 17021	3250	2960	2638	2440	3519	2919	2318	1983		100	0	−2.4	−9.5
										180	+0.9	+0.6	−6.8
										200	+1.2	0	−5.8
7x64 150 gr/9.7 g 17013	2890	2598	2329	2113	2779	2449	1807	1487		100	0	−3.3	−12.5
										180	+1.2	−0.8	−8.8
										200	+1.7	0	−7.5
7x64 175 gr/11.3 g 17015	2725	2516	2339	2198	2884	2460	2126	1878		100	0	−3.6	−12.7
										180	+1.4	−0.9	−8.5
										200	+1.8	0	−7.2
280 Rem. 150 gr/9.7 g 17050	2900	2683	2475	2277	2802	2398	2041	1727		100	0	−3.4	−12.4
										180	+1.2	−0.8	−8.6
										200	+1.7	0	−7.4
7.5x55 Swiss 180 gr/11.6 g 17511	2650	2441	2248	2056	2792	2380	2020	1690		100	0	−4.3	−15.3
										180	+1.6	−1.0	−10.4
										200	+2.1	0	−8.9
30 US Carbine 110 gr/7.1 g 17621	1970	1595	1300	1090	948	622	413	290		100	0	−12.4	−45.7
										130	+1.5	−9.3	−41.1
										200	+6.2	0	−27.0
7.62 Russian 180 gr/11.6 g 17634	2625	2415	2222	2030	2749	2326	1970	1644		100	0	−4.4	−15.7
										180	+1.7	−1.1	−10.7
										200	+2.2	0	−9.1
30—06 130 gr/8.4 g 17640	3205	2876	2561	2263	2966	2388	1894	1479		100	0	−2.7	−10.8
										180	+1.0	−0.7	−7.8
										200	+1.4	0	−6.7
30—06 146 gr/9.5 g 17651	2772	2549	2336	2133	2485	2102	1765	1472		100	0	−3.9	−14.3
										180	+1.5	−1.0	−9.9
										200	+2.0	0	−8.4
30—06 150 gr/9.7 g 17643	2970	2680	2402	2141	2943	2393	1922	1527		100	0	−3.4	−12.9
										180	+1.3	−0.9	−9.1
										200	+1.7	0	−7.8
303 British 150 gr/9.7 g 17712	2720	2440	2170	1930	2465	1983	1569	1241		100	0	−4.4	−16.3
										180	+1.7	−1.1	−11.3
										200	+2.2	0	−9.7
303 British 180 gr/11.6 g 17713	2540	2340	2147	1965	2579	2189	1843	1544		100	0	−4.9	−17.3
										130	+0.6	−3.7	−15.6
										200	+2.4	0	−10.0

STALKING DO'S AND DON'TS

DO 1   Spy carefully all ground.

2   Make a mental note of all deer.

3   Select a prominent mark above all deer which can be recognised from other positions so as to locate the deer.

4   Decide which deer to shoot and plan a stalking route.

5   Keep close together during the stalk and do what the stalker does when and where he does it.

6   If part of the stalk is to be in sight of the deer, choose the alternative route (if any) where movement in sight is at the maximum distance from the deer.

7   Never hurry except in very special circumstances.

8   Always make use of the best rest and firing position available.

9   Take plenty of cartridges (15–20). Things can go wrong eg if the telescope sight gets knocked.

10   Carry a compass, whistle, crepe bandage (for sprained ankles', and a small roll of sticking plaster (useful for repairing many things as well as you!) as a minimum first aid.

DON'T 1   Go over sky-lines: go round hillocks instead.

2   Ever shoot unless the rifle is absolutely steady. If it is not, it is far better to try to get a better rest, or even to have no shot, than to risk wounding.

3   Jump up after the shot: still less shout in joy. Always let the remaining deer go quietly away.

4   Hurry after the shot. Reload and watch the deer you have shot even if apparently dead.

5   Crawl with a large bag etc on your back: it sticks up in view of the deer far more than you think!

6   Move the deer unless it is unavoidable.

7   Get a stag up which is lying, so as to present a better shot, until you have to do so—eg when cold or cramp are setting in. When you do, do it slowly making a small noise at first, then gradually a little more.

8   Let a telescope glass etc 'flash' in the sunlight.

9 Ever put the rifle away in its cover after shooting a stag until it has been bled. Very occasionally one is not as dead as you thought.

10 Leave part of the party behind without full instructions on how long to wait, what to do then etc.

11 Forget that waiting is a very boring and often cold and wet job—keep it to a minimum.

12 Forget to replace the bolt after cleaning out the oil in the morning.

INDEX